YOUTH
IN
CANADIAN
POLITICS

~

This is Volume 8 in a series of studies commissioned as part of the research program of the Royal Commission on Electoral Reform and Party Financing

YOUTH
IN
CANADIAN
POLITICS
PARTICIPATION AND
INVOLVEMENT

~

Kathy Megyery
Editor

Volume 8 of the Research Studies

ROYAL COMMISSION ON ELECTORAL REFORM
AND PARTY FINANCING
AND CANADA COMMUNICATION GROUP –
PUBLISHING, SUPPLY AND SERVICES CANADA

DUNDURN PRESS
TORONTO AND OXFORD

© Minister of Supply and Services Canada, 1991
Printed and bound in Canada
ISBN 1-55002-104-4
ISSN 1188-2743
Catalogue No. Z1-1989/2-41-8E

Published by Dundurn Press Limited in cooperation with the Royal
Commission on Electoral Reform and Party Financing and Canada
Communication Group – Publishing, Supply and Services Canada.

Canadian Cataloguing in Publication Data

Main entry under title:
Youth in Canadian Politics

(Research studies ; 8)
Issued also in French under title: Les Jeunes et la vie politique au Canada.
ISBN 1-55002-104-4

1. Youth – Canada – Political activity. I. Megyery, Kathy, 1962 – .
II. Canada. Royal Commission on Electoral Reform and Party Financing.
III. Series: Research studies (Canada. Royal Commission on Electoral Reform
and Party Financing) ; 8.

HQ799.2.P6Y68 1991   305.23′5′0971   C91-090520-7

Dundurn Press Limited
2181 Queen Street East
Suite 301
Toronto, Canada
M4E 1E5

Dundurn Distribution
73 Lime Walk
Headington
Oxford, England
OX3 7AD

CONTENTS

~

3. LOWERING THE VOTING AGE TO 16 95

JON H. PAMMETT AND JOHN MYLES

TABLES

1. TO WHAT EXTENT ARE TODAY'S YOUNG PEOPLE INTERESTED IN POLITICS? INQUIRIES AMONG 16- TO 24-YEAR-OLDS

3. LOWERING THE VOTING AGE TO 16

FOREWORD

~

THE ROYAL COMMISSION on Electoral Reform and Party Financing was established in November 1989. Our mandate was to inquire into and report on the appropriate principles and process that should govern the election of members of the House of Commons and the financing of political parties and candidates' campaigns. To conduct such a comprehensive examination of Canada's electoral system, we held extensive public consultations and developed a research program designed to ensure that our recommendations would be guided by an independent foundation of empirical inquiry and analysis.

The Commission's in-depth review of the electoral system was the first of its kind in Canada's history of electoral democracy. It was dictated largely by the major constitutional, social and technological changes of the past several decades, which have transformed Canadian society, and their concomitant influence on Canadians' expectations of the political process itself. In particular, the adoption in 1982 of the *Canadian Charter of Rights and Freedoms* has heightened Canadians' awareness of their democratic and political rights and of the way they are served by the electoral system.

The importance of electoral reform cannot be overemphasized. As the Commission's work proceeded, Canadians became increasingly preoccupied with constitutional issues that have the potential to change the nature of Confederation. No matter what their beliefs or political allegiances in this continuing debate, Canadians agree that constitutional change must be achieved in the context of fair and democratic processes. We cannot complacently assume that our current electoral process will always meet this standard or that it leaves no room for improvement. Parliament and the national government must be seen as legitimate; electoral reform can both enhance the stature of national political institutions and reinforce their ability to define the future of our country in ways that command Canadians' respect and confidence and promote the national interest.

In carrying out our mandate, we remained mindful of the importance of protecting our democratic heritage, while at the same time balancing it against the emerging values that are injecting a new dynamic into the electoral system. If our system is to reflect the realities of Canadian political life, then reform requires more than mere tinkering with electoral laws and practices.

Our broad mandate challenged us to explore a full range of options. We commissioned more than 100 research studies, to be published in a 23-volume collection. In the belief that our electoral laws must measure up to the very best contemporary practice, we examined election-related laws and processes in all of our provinces and territories and studied comparable legislation and processes in established democracies around the world. This unprecedented array of empirical study and expert opinion made a vital contribution to our deliberations. We made every effort to ensure that the research was both intellectually rigorous and of practical value. All studies were subjected to peer review, and many of the authors discussed their preliminary findings with members of the political and academic communities at national symposiums on major aspects of the electoral system.

The Commission placed the research program under the able and inspired direction of Dr. Peter Aucoin, Professor of Political Science and Public Administration at Dalhousie University. We are confident that the efforts of Dr. Aucoin, together with those of the research coordinators and scholars whose work appears in this and other volumes, will continue to be of value to historians, political scientists, parliamentarians and policy makers, as well as to thoughtful Canadians and the international community.

Along with the other Commissioners, I extend my sincere gratitude to the entire Commission staff for their dedication and commitment. I also wish to thank the many people who participated in our symposiums for their valuable contributions, as well as the members of the research and practitioners' advisory groups whose counsel significantly aided our undertaking.

Pierre Lortie
Chairman

INTRODUCTION

~

THE ROYAL COMMISSION'S research program constituted a comprehensive and detailed examination of the Canadian electoral process. The scope of the research, undertaken to assist Commissioners in their deliberations, was dictated by the broad mandate given to the Commission.

The objective of the research program was to provide Commissioners with a full account of the factors that have shaped our electoral democracy. This dictated, first and foremost, a focus on federal electoral law, but our inquiries also extended to the Canadian constitution, including the institutions of parliamentary government, the practices of political parties, the mass media and nonpartisan political organizations, as well as the decision-making role of the courts with respect to the constitutional rights of citizens. Throughout, our research sought to introduce a historical perspective in order to place the contemporary experience within the Canadian political tradition.

We recognized that neither our consideration of the factors shaping Canadian electoral democracy nor our assessment of reform proposals would be as complete as necessary if we failed to examine the experiences of Canadian provinces and territories and of other democracies. Our research program thus emphasized comparative dimensions in relation to the major subjects of inquiry.

Our research program involved, in addition to the work of the Commission's research coordinators, analysts and support staff, over 200 specialists from 28 universities in Canada, from the private sector and, in a number of cases, from abroad. Specialists in political science constituted the majority of our researchers, but specialists in law, economics, management, computer sciences, ethics, sociology and communications, among other disciplines, were also involved.

In addition to the preparation of research studies for the Commission, our research program included a series of research seminars, symposiums and workshops. These meetings brought together the Commissioners, researchers, representatives from the political parties, media personnel and others with practical experience in political parties, electoral politics and public affairs. These meetings provided not only a forum for discussion of the various subjects of the Commission's mandate, but also an opportunity for our research to be assessed by those with an intimate knowledge of the world of political practice.

These public reviews of our research were complemented by internal and external assessments of each research report by persons qualified in the area; such assessments were completed prior to our decision to publish any study in the series of research volumes.

The Research Branch of the Commission was divided into several areas, with the individual research projects in each area assigned to the research coordinators as follows:

F. Leslie Seidle	Political Party and Election Finance
Herman Bakvis	Political Parties
Kathy Megyery	Women, Ethno-Cultural Groups and Youth
David Small	Redistribution; Electoral Boundaries; Voter Registration
Janet Hiebert	Party Ethics
Michael Cassidy	Democratic Rights; Election Administration
Robert A. Milen	Aboriginal Electoral Participation and Representation
Frederick J. Fletcher	Mass Media and Broadcasting in Elections
David Mac Donald (Assistant Research Coordinator)	Direct Democracy

These coordinators identified appropriate specialists to undertake research, managed the projects and prepared them for publication. They also organized the seminars, symposiums and workshops in their research areas and were responsible for preparing presentations and briefings to help the Commission in its deliberations and decision making. Finally, they participated in drafting the Final Report of the Commission.

On behalf of the Commission, I welcome the opportunity to thank the following for their generous assistance in producing these research studies – a project that required the talents of many individuals.

In performing their duties, the research coordinators made a notable contribution to the work of the Commission. Despite the pressures of tight deadlines, they worked with unfailing good humour and the utmost congeniality. I thank all of them for their consistent support and cooperation.

In particular, I wish to express my gratitude to Leslie Seidle, senior research coordinator, who supervised our research analysts and support staff in Ottawa. His diligence, commitment and professionalism not only set high standards, but also proved contagious. I am grateful to Kathy Megyery, who performed a similar function in Montreal with equal aplomb and skill. Her enthusiasm and dedication inspired us all.

On behalf of the research coordinators and myself, I wish to thank our research analysts: Daniel Arsenault, Eric Bertram, Cécile Boucher, Peter Constantinou, Yves Denoncourt, David Docherty, Luc Dumont, Jane Dunlop, Scott Evans, Véronique Garneau, Keith Heintzman, Paul Holmes, Hugh Mellon, Cheryl D. Mitchell, Donald Padget, Alain Pelletier, Dominique Tremblay and Lisa Young. The Research Branch was strengthened by their ability to carry out research in a wide variety of areas, their intellectual curiosity and their team spirit.

The work of the research coordinators and analysts was greatly facilitated by the professional skills and invaluable cooperation of Research Branch staff members: Paulette LeBlanc, who, as administrative assistant, managed the flow of research projects; Hélène Leroux, secretary to the research coordinators, who produced briefing material for the Commissioners and who, with Lori Nazar, assumed responsibility for monitoring the progress of research projects in the latter stages of our work; Kathleen McBride and her assistant Natalie Brose, who created and maintained the database of briefs and hearings transcripts; and Richard Herold and his assistant Susan Dancause, who were responsible for our research library. Jacinthe Séguin and Cathy Tucker also deserve thanks – in addition to their duties as receptionists, they assisted in a variety of ways to help us meet deadlines.

We were extremely fortunate to obtain the research services of first-class specialists from the academic and private sectors. Their contributions are found in this and the other 22 published research volumes. We thank them for the quality of their work and for their willingness to contribute and to meet our tight deadlines.

Our research program also benefited from the counsel of Jean-Marc Hamel, Special Adviser to the Chairman of the Commission and former

Chief Electoral Officer of Canada, whose knowledge and experience proved invaluable.

In addition, numerous specialists assessed our research studies. Their assessments not only improved the quality of our published studies, but also provided us with much-needed advice on many issues. In particular, we wish to single out professors Donald Blake, Janine Brodie, Alan Cairns, Kenneth Carty, John Courtney, Peter Desbarats, Jane Jenson, Richard Johnston, Vincent Lemieux, Terry Morley and Joseph Wearing, as well as Ms. Beth Symes.

Producing such a large number of studies in less than a year requires a mastery of the skills and logistics of publishing. We were fortunate to be able to count on the Commission's Director of Communications, Richard Rochefort, and Assistant Director, Hélène Papineau. They were ably supported by the Communications staff: Patricia Burden, Louise Dagenais, Caroline Field, Claudine Labelle, France Langlois, Lorraine Maheux, Ruth McVeigh, Chantal Morissette, Sylvie Patry, Jacques Poitras and Claudette Rouleau-O'Toole.

To bring the project to fruition, the Commission also called on specialized contractors. We are deeply grateful for the services of Ann McCoomb (references and fact checking); Marthe Lemery, Pierre Chagnon and the staff of Communications Com'ça (French quality control); Norman Bloom, Pamela Riseborough and associates of B&B Editorial Consulting (English adaptation and quality control); and Mado Reid (French production). Al Albania and his staff at Acart Graphics designed the studies and produced some 2 400 tables and figures.

The Commission's research reports constitute Canada's largest publishing project of 1991. Successful completion of the project required close cooperation between the public and private sectors. In the public sector, we especially acknowledge the excellent service of the Privy Council unit of the Translation Bureau, Department of the Secretary of State of Canada, under the direction of Michel Parent, and our contacts Ruth Steele and Terry Denovan of the Canada Communication Group, Department of Supply and Services.

The Commission's co-publisher for the research studies was Dundurn Press of Toronto, whose exceptional service is gratefully acknowledged. Wilson & Lafleur of Montreal, working with the Centre de Documentation Juridique du Québec, did equally admirable work in preparing the French version of the studies.

Teams of editors, copy editors and proofreaders worked diligently under stringent deadlines with the Commission and the publishers to prepare some 20 000 pages of manuscript for design, typesetting and printing. The work of these individuals, whose names are listed elsewhere in this volume, was greatly appreciated.

Our acknowledgements extend to the contributions of the Commission's Executive Director, Guy Goulard, and the administration and executive support teams: Maurice Lacasse, Denis Lafrance and Steve Tremblay (finance); Thérèse Lacasse and Mary Guy-Shea (personnel); Cécile Desforges (assistant to the Executive Director); Marie Dionne (administration); Anna Bevilacqua (records); and support staff members Michelle Bélanger, Roch Langlois, Michel Lauzon, Jean Mathieu, David McKay and Pierrette McMurtie, as well as Denise Miquelon and Christiane Séguin of the Montreal office.

A special debt of gratitude is owed to Marlène Girard, assistant to the Chairman. Her ability to supervise the logistics of the Commission's work amid the tight schedules of the Chairman and Commissioners contributed greatly to the completion of our task.

I also wish to express my deep gratitude to my own secretary, Liette Simard. Her superb administrative skills and great patience brought much-appreciated order to my penchant for the chaotic workstyle of academe. She also assumed responsibility for the administrative coordination of revisions to the final drafts of volumes 1 and 2 of the Commission's Final Report. I owe much to her efforts and assistance.

Finally, on behalf of the research coordinators and myself, I wish to thank the Chairman, Pierre Lortie, the members of the Commission, Pierre Fortier, Robert Gabor, William Knight and Lucie Pépin, and former members Elwood Cowley and Senator Donald Oliver. We are honoured to have worked with such an eminent and thoughtful group of Canadians, and we have benefited immensely from their knowledge and experience. In particular, we wish to acknowledge the creativity, intellectual rigour and energy our Chairman brought to our task. His unparalleled capacity to challenge, to bring out the best in us, was indeed inspiring.

Peter Aucoin
Director of Research

PREFACE

~

THERE IS A widespread perception on the part of social commentators that young people are indifferent or even hostile to the contemporary practice of politics. They appear to have opted out to pursue their own largely self-centred interests, in sharp contrast to the commitment of a previous generation of activists. According to this view, youth has espoused the conservative values of the age and has forsaken its natural role as critic of the political establishment. However, another interpretation points to indications that youth has been developing new forms of social activism. The commitment of youth to, for example, the environmental movement is broader-based and less partisan and ideological than student movements of the previous period. This argument suggests that we are witnessing the emergence of a new type of politics. Which interpretation holds the truth?

In their study, based on the results of surveys and interviews with Quebec high school and university students, Raymond Hudon and colleagues demarcate these general assessments. They find both wanting to some extent. They agree that there is deep suspicion of current political parties and institutions among the young. They discover, however, that there is also considerable acknowledgement of the value of politics. At the same time, however, the acknowledgement is expressed in traditional terms for the most part, and the researchers do not find widespread evidence to support the position that youth are moving to a completely new approach to politics. Finding considerable diversity in young people's social and political attitudes, they conclude that youth cannot readily be identified with a homogeneous set of attitudes. Perhaps it is only a methodological imperative that seeks a single view that can be claimed to characterize youth.

Hudon also warns us of the myths that have developed surrounding the student movement of the sixties. Studies indicate that only a small percentage of students were truly committed at that time. Moreover, even in those days, the path to political and social action took many forms. The Hudon study suggests that it is unduly constraining to insist on a single form of activity as an indicator of political involvement. Rather, the political process itself should support multiple approaches. In this context, they suggest supportive policies such as greater political education and lowering the voting age to encourage participation and feelings of political efficacy among youth.

The issue of the voting age is the topic of the other two studies in this volume. In the first, Patrice Garant assesses the constitutional implications of retaining or lowering the voting age. With the adoption of the *Canadian Charter of Rights and Freedoms,* legislators no longer have complete discretion in setting the voting age; they must ensure that the legislation governing the voting age respects the provisions of the Charter. The study provides a careful assessment of this issue by questioning whether the age of majority should coincide with the age to vote and by examining what powers in the criminal, social, economic and educational realms are granted under various statutes to young people below the age of majority. The author goes on to examine the relevant jurisprudence in the United States and Canada for indications of how the courts might interpret the Charter in relation to the voting age. Garant concludes that ultimately the decision about where to set the voting age is somewhat arbitrary and reflects the judgement of a society about when young people reach political maturity.

In the final study of the volume, Jon Pammett and John Myles examine the arguments surrounding the question of lowering the voting age to 16. They ground their arguments in 1969 when the voting age was lowered from 21 to 18 and suggest that many of the reasons that were advanced for lowering the voting age to 18 remain the same in the current debate. The two central perspectives are whether younger people have the political maturity to cast a rational and informed vote and whether younger people who are already entrusted with a number of "adult" responsibilities should be denied the right to vote. Pammett and Myles also suggest, along the lines of Hudon et al., that a lower voting age could have a significant impact on improving political education in Canada, because young people would then be involved in the political process while still attending high school.

My most sincere thanks go to Peter Aucoin, Director of Research, for his invaluable guidance and unfailingly cheerful support.

Kathy Megyery
Research Coordinator

YOUTH
IN
CANADIAN
POLITICS

~

1

TO WHAT EXTENT ARE TODAY'S YOUNG PEOPLE INTERESTED IN POLITICS?

Inquiries among 16- to 24-Year-Olds

~

Raymond Hudon
Bernard Fournier
Louis Métivier
with the assistance of
Benoît-Paul Hébert

THE POLITICIZATION OF TODAY'S YOUNG PEOPLE

THE AIM OF this study is to describe the nature of young people's attitudes toward politics as well as to convey the extent that they are motivated by or even interested in politics. The issue is timely, and not simply for the reason that today's youth will shape tomorrow's politics. In recent years, there have been numerous studies which have thoroughly analysed the general values and attitudes of young people 15 to 29 years of age, including their specific responses to the current political scene. Surveys (*L'Actualité* 1989; Canadian Youth Foundation 1989), essays and sociological studies (Dumont 1986; *L'Action nationale* 1990) all present a paradoxical portrait of young people in this domain. It appears that their perception of politics does not correspond to their day-to-day practice; they may cherish a political ideal but their attitudes are more practical than utopian; they are reluctant to join established political parties and prefer rather to participate in the activities of humanitarian associations.

Given these basic features of young people's attitudes toward politics, it is perhaps not surprising that commentators have drawn virtually contradictory interpretations. For some observers, young people are simply apolitical and exhibit behaviour that, far from challenging the established order, seeks a closer integration. Others interpret their behaviour as profoundly political in its search for a "new politics" which differs from traditional political activity. *Apoliticism* versus *new politics* is the focal point of the debate now animating studies on young people. Yet it should be realized that both interpretations, however contradictory, share the perspective that youth is – or ought to be – a period of political and social protest.

This type of discussion has its problems and pitfalls. To begin, what interpretation should be given to the concept of "youth" used by sociologists to classify the comportment of specified individuals? Like any other major sociological category, this category does not constitute a given naturally homogeneous group. The notion of "young people" encompasses very different experiences which depend on the circumstances of the individual concerned. There are marked differences between the student and the young working person, and again between a young person from a privileged background and one initially disadvantaged. Moreover, as observed in a report submitted to the French government in the early 1980s, these differences are often greater among the young than between them and their parents (Schwartz 1981).

Nonetheless, one should not jump to the conclusion that the expression "youth" is only "an extraordinary abuse of language" (Bourdieu 1980, 145) not reflecting any sociological reality whatsoever. The expression must be taken to refer to a transition period whose length depends on the individual, the period in question and the particular context as well as any relevant cultural practices. Nor must the behaviour associated with this period be arbitrarily generalized to cover all individuals of the same physiological age (as for example, "15- to 24-year-olds think that ..."). Such a generalization would never be found in a study describing the behaviour of individuals who happened to be adults!

Ideally, there should be more precise indicators relating to the transition between infancy and adulthood as actually lived (the first job, the first apartment away from home and so on) which could be used to characterize "youth." It is only through a projection of these lived experiences that one can justify in talking of "youth" the use of such categories as "16–24 years of age" and "15–30 years of age."

Given that the individual behaviour of "youth" cannot be generalized, one can hardly link a given age with a designated degree of political consciousness. Even if it is acknowledged, as in the study by

Rezsohazy (1983, 7) on the values of young people, that some may sometimes want to "remake the world" or to "replace history with a tabula rasa," it must never be forgotten that these attitudes are manifested for each individual in diverse, even contradictory, ways.

These reservations have led us to conclude that any study of the political behaviour of, for example, 16- to 24-year-olds should not be limited, as is too often the case, to an analysis of the primary tendency that emerges during a survey or study.[1] One should always consider all the significant groups of responses to illustrate the diversity of the opinions canvassed. Even if 60 percent of young people indicate that they are not interested in politics, a substantial group thinks the opposite and should not be ignored by the research analyst. It must also be kept in mind that since any such breakdown can only vary as the study's diagnostic indicators are changed, one can readily revise one's views on the true degree of politicization of young people.

So, to play with words, if the interest of today's young in politics appears somewhat measured, there remains the question of the measurement of this attitude. Furthermore, the assessment of any social attitude does depend on the points of reference chosen by the analysis. In response to this problem of the relativity of reference, this study will consider some in order to illustrate possible approaches. To this end, the results of two recent inquiries with differing research methods will be used. One, undertaken with the aid of a grant from the Social Sciences and Humanities Research Council of Canada, comprised interviews with 75 students at Université Laval; the other involved a closed questionnaire distributed to 1 008 secondary students in the classroom (at seven schools in the Quebec City area and one near Drummondville).[2]

The first two parts of this study will draw on these prior investigations. The first uses the Laval study to compare differing discourse on politics: what has been maintained about the politicization of the young? what are young people actually saying in this regard? In the second part of this study, we shall see that even though the high school students surveyed appeared not to be interested in politics, this attitude in no way reflects poorly on their social commitment. On the contrary, young people today participate in numerous different groups, a sign perhaps of a new period of social activism.

A final preliminary remark: neither our methodological concerns nor the nuances of our presentation should create the impression that there is nothing that the older generations can do to encourage young people's interest in politics. The third part of this study takes up this issue and, among other recommendations, proposes that 16-year-olds be given the right to vote. By no means a panacea, this proposal would encourage, at the very least, debate on bringing politics and its practice back into public favour. If adults had to let young people develop their capacity for action, it would follow that adults themselves would become more interested and involved in political matters.

THE POLITICIZATION OF YOUNG PEOPLE: ASSESSMENT AND REALITY

Any discussion concerning the politicization of young people must be placed in an historical context. The 1980s began in a climate of economic crisis, clouded by high unemployment which affected young people particularly hard.[3] The decade is also noteworthy for various social trends. Western societies are ageing, and the social and political power of young people is shifting toward the elderly. Moreover, to find their place in the world, young people must overcome various barriers established by those who already hold positions in our society.[4] Finally, this generation of young people has grown up under governments that were forced to revise their agendas as a result of the "defeat of the grand myths" propounded by their parents, the generation of the 1960s.

Pursuing the Spirit of a Generation

Apolitical and Indifferent ...
According to some observers, young people seem to be enveloped in quiet resignation, having abandoned the ideals that mobilized their parents' generation. Some deplore this passivity of the "so what" generation. It appears to many observers that collective action in support of social reform is no longer fashionable and that self-interest prevails. At best, according to this perspective, young people are struggling to get by in difficult times, as the 21st session of the Unesco General Conference noted in the early 1980s: "The focus of concern of young people now centres around everyday life and the struggle simply to get by which is characteristic of hard times" (Unesco 1981, 21).

There is much polemic directed against this new generation whose scepticism, pragmatism and individualism are stigmatized as conservative values in stark opposition to the liberal values of their predecessors.[5] "What a striking contrast in 20 years!" notes one writer (Carraud 1989, 9). On the eve of International Youth Year in 1985, some were quite amused at the idea of reserving a year for a group which, a decade earlier, would never have expected anyone to give it a voice of its own.

... Committed, on Its Own Terms
Some commentators offer an entirely different interpretation of this

generation and see evidence not so much of a flight from the great battles but of a profound desire for reflection and a new start. Far from selfishly conservative, the young are committed in new, less constraining ways: structured organizations are consciously rejected in favour of independent individual action.

This assessment generally dominated a symposium organized at Université Laval in 1985 by young political science students, to the great consternation of speakers who did their utmost to elaborate the notions of commitment and politicization in traditional terms. One young participant summed up this broader alternative view of politics in a critical response to a presentation by one of the symposium's organizers:

> We have been talking about politicization, except that you have not defined what you mean by politicization and, indeed, I have the impression that you are referring to traditional politicization – that is, involvement in a political party, anti-government demonstrations and so on. You have not given any other definitions, which has perhaps led you to reject out of hand involvement in community groups. Women's shelters and youth centres are real. There are young people who are organizing themselves to live differently in ways more individualistic but at the same time more collective: cooperatives are becoming increasingly widespread. (AÉÉSPUL 1986, 37)

According to this perspective, young people are not rejecting militancy: they are changing the very concept. Consider for example the following observation in an article that appeared in *Le Devoir*: "Militancy is not dead, but it is no longer practised in the same way. Militants in the 1980s want to fight for something small, temporary and energizing, rather than fight for big, noble, complex and exhausting principles" (Martine d'Amours, quoted in Petrowski 1985, 37).

Zarka (1983) explains this phenomenon in the same way, emphasizing that young people are not rejecting politics but are moving toward another kind of politics by participating in different types of groups:

> We are entitled to ask whether the expression "rejection of politics" captures the entire problem well or whether we are witnessing a non-traditional response to a politics that no longer corresponds to the new sensibilities, if not in fact the birth of a new way of engaging or wanting to engage in politics.

In France this interpretation has seemed quite legitimate and was supported by the demonstrations of high school and university students during November and December of 1986. According to Joffrin (1987, 161): "The movement demonstrated the existence of a new way of engaging in politics and of an enormous reserve of good will and ability to mobilize." Young people seem to be withdrawing from politics as it is now practised, a caricature of democracy, to focus on a new politics "centred on people" (Touraine 1986).

Whether one accepts the first or second assessment of the nature and degree of politicization of today's young people, the 1980s did see the demise of one significant feature of the earlier generation: "Indoctrination and big demonstrations are over and done with" (Blouin 1984, 41). Henceforth, young people are moved to action by everyday matters and not by great, abstract, utopian ideals (Carraud 1989, 20). Young people, as Camilleri and Tapia have written (1983, 79), "look critically ... at society and the functioning of certain of its institutions, particularly the political institutions." They appear to forgo involvement in traditional organizations, "tentacular" and divorced from reality, to tackle concrete problems within small groups, such as associations for the defence of human rights.

In a phrase, we seem to be in the presence of a "quietly lucid generation" (Dumas et al. 1982).

Politics as Seen by Students at Université Laval

Overall, the Université Laval students interviewed during our 1989 study[6] confirm the belief that young people today are not really interested in politics. This opinion is more pronounced among male than

Table 1.1
Overall opinion of students about young people's interest in politics, by sex

	Statement A[a]		Statement B		Statement C		Total	
	%	N	%	N	%	N	%	N
Male students	66	29	16	7	18	8	100	44
Female students	58	18	32	10	10	3	100	31

Note: Total sample, 1989 inquiry: 75 Université Laval students.

[a]Statement A: Young people display no or very little interest in politics a) because politics is "dull," "we can't change anything" and young people are not represented; b) because young people have other values and other concerns such as "getting the most out of life" and finding a job.

Statement B: "Appearances to the contrary" young people are interested in politics, even if they do not participate; some believe that young people have not become accustomed to politics, others that there is no place for them in the political process.

Statement C: "That depends!" Some young people are extensively involved, but most are uninterested; it is also thought that people take an interest in politics when it directly affects them or when some benefit is to be gained from it.

Table 1.2
Overall opinion of students about young people's interest in politics, by field of study

	Statement A[a]		Statement B		Statement C		Total	
	%	N	%	N	%	N	%	N
Political science	72	18	12	3	16	4	100	25
Social sciences	64	16	28	7	8	2	100	25
Other faculties	52	13	28	7	20	5	100	25

Note: Total sample, 1989 inquiry: 75 Université Laval students.
[a]See Table 1.1.

female students (table 1.1) and among those studying political science (table 1.2). It is perhaps interesting to suggest that students in this discipline are in a better position to reflect on this issue.[7]

In the minds of several of those interviewed, however, this absence of interest in politics is not based on some sort of negligence or laziness on the part of young people. Rather, it is the result of the image and practice of current politics. Why become involved in such futile exercises which don't seem to address the real problems? A 21-year-old male political science student summed up the opinion of many young people:

> I think politics is *deadly dull*. Politicians give us nothing. The biggest debate at the moment concerns store opening hours! And, when you're not sure of finding a job after three years of university, I can understand why people first make sure the boat is afloat before looking at the colour of the sails. Young people are not very interested in politics, but there are many reasons why.

Some students readily acknowledge that other young people are interested in politics. But the behaviour of those working within the current political process is often seen in as negative a light as politics itself. According to a female political science student:

> One group of [young people] seems to get involved in the game, and the others think it is a joke. Some of them take it seriously and wear a red tie if they're Liberal ... I feel closer to the others. We don't call it the "political scene" for nothing. I am working at the Ministry of the Environment [in a training program] and when we look at what's happening at the upper echelons, all we see are dinners and cocktail parties.

These attitudes corroborate the view that the majority of young people reject politics. However, by comparing this initial, mainly negative, perception with the students' conception of politics, one can develop a different and more subtle picture of their interest in politics.[8]

Certainly, for the majority, the conception of politics is general and traditional and relates to the process of organizing and managing the affairs of society. Politics involves governing, the determination of policy direction and the establishment of laws and rules. For these young people, politics is clearly something external, a stage where they can watch the political actors perform their roles of governing and law making. For a 22-year-old female psychology student, a politician is "someone who decides for the majority, or at least tries to. They decide what we do, even when some of us don't agree."

But others see a circus which offers a spectacle of balances of power and struggles for prestige. For one 23-year-old female political science student: "Quite frankly, I think politics is a big joke. In my view, now that I'm completely disillusioned, it's a packet of dreams that have been swept aside"; another 23-year-old male student in political science suggests: "[Politics] is a power game ... a game of interests, a struggle that occasionally defies all logic; it's somewhat discouraging. At present, it's really no more than that."

There is also a group of students which conceives politics in much broader terms. For one 22-year-old male political science student, politics is synonymous with ideology or with the big picture: "[Politics] is about defending your goals, defending what you like." On this approach, politics resembles more an attitude or style of behaviour rather than an arena reserved for a few decision makers. For one 24-year-old female student in physical education, politics concerns to be sure "the government, those to whom we have given the right to govern at the municipal, provincial, and federal levels ... [But] we can also make political gestures every day, for example, by taking old newspapers to be recycled."

These diverse definitions, nevertheless, are rarely mutually exclusive nor are the opinions well demarcated. Even if it becomes extremely difficult and highly constraining to quantify the variety of opinion, the tables (tables 1.3, 1.4) indicating the broad trends do reveal the extent of the diversity.

Nearly 40 percent of respondents regard politics as a way to manage society; this view is pronounced among young women and political science students and represents in our view a rather neutral, even indifferent, attitude to the subject. But we must not overlook the fact that of all the students surveyed the political science students also had the most positive opinions of politics: that politics is important because it

Table 1.3
Overall opinion of students about politics, by sex

	Indifferent / neutral[a]		Negative		Critical		Positive		Total	
	%	N	%	N	%	N	%	N	%	N
Male students	25	11	16	7	27	12	32	14	100	44
Female students	55	17	16	5	16	5	13	4	100	31

Note: Total sample, 1989 inquiry: 75 Université Laval students.

[a]*Indifferent/neutral:* In this group, politics does not arouse any particular feeling. Respondents perceive politics in terms of institutions, e.g., elections, elected officials, parties and legislation, or as a sort of machine that manages society and that, as expected, occasionally fails.

Negative: These respondents perceive politics in largely pejorative terms, i.e., as being artificial, deceitful, abstract, characterized by favouritism, promises, problems and so on.

Critical: Respondents in this group see politics in a positive light, if only in theory, but actually feel that it does not live up to its or their aspirations.

Positive: This group is made up of respondents who are enthusiastic about politics. They feel that politics concerns and affects the lives of everyone, enables people to make themselves heard, to settle conflicts and helps society progress.

Table 1.4
Overall opinion of students about politics, by field of study

	Indifferent / neutral[a]		Negative		Critical		Positive		Total	
	%	N	%	N	%	N	%	N	%	N
Political science	48	12	12	3	8	2	32	8	100	25
Social sciences	28	7	28	7	28	7	16	4	100	25
Other faculties	36	9	8	2	32	8	24	6	100	25

Note: Total sample, 1989 inquiry: 75 Université Laval students.

[a]Indifferent/neutral, Negative, Critical, Positive, see table 1.3.

affects everyone; that it enables people to make themselves heard in society; that it helps resolve conflicts and that it advances our society. Along with the political science students, we found that more male than female students subscribed to this positive view of politics.

It is not surprising that we also found some negative respondents who persisted in the view that politics was artificial, deceitful, abstract and dishonest. However, this group was smaller than anticipated, particularly if we removed those who saw the positive side of politics and found it a necessary component of social existence in spite of their reservations. These reservations related to the feeling that politics does not presently satisfy their expectations (regarding the behaviour of politicians, the issues under discussion and so on).

Indeed, this attitude is more widespread than the figures in tables 1.3 and 1.4 would suggest. For the students interviewed at Université Laval, the criticism of politics did not amount to wholesale condemnation nor even to a personal distancing from political affairs. In fact, most respondents believe that young people ought to take an interest in politics (tables 1.5, 1.6).

Up to this point, and based solely on student discourse, it is possible to discern a diversity of opinion that should temper general assessments regarding young people's interest in politics. First, it is true that a good number have a relatively neutral, even indifferent, opinion of politics, and that others, in rejecting politics, see only trickery and deceit.

Table 1.5

Breakdown of students' opinions on the advantages for young people of taking an interest in politics, by sex

	Statement A[a]		Statement B		Statement C		Total	
	%	N	%	N	%	N	%	N
Male students	57	25	43	19	0	0	100	44
Female students	71	22	19	6	10	3	100	31

Note: Total sample, 1989 inquiry: 75 Université Laval students.

[a]*Statement A:* There are obvious advantages to taking an interest in politics because "our future depends on it" (variant A1: so that young people are heard and account is taken of them; variant A2: to take a critical look at elected officials and oversee the manner in which problems are dealt with; variant A3: to introduce new ideas and initiate changes that benefit everyone).

Statement B: There are no disadvantages to taking an interest in politics, but the advantages are not obvious (variant B1: keeping abreast of current affairs makes it possible to prepare for the day when young people will be responsible for these matters; variant B2: there are many possible advantages, such as jobs, influence, contacts and so on, but nothing is certain; there is some doubt about the efficacy of political involvement).

Statement C: There is no apparent advantage to taking an interest in politics.

Table 1.6

Breakdown of students' opinions on the advantages for young people of taking an interest in politics, by field of study

	Statement A[a]		Statement B		Statement C		Total	
	%	N	%	N	%	N	%	N
Political science	72	18	28	7	0	0	100	25
Social sciences	64	16	28	7	8	2	100	25
Other faculties	52	13	44	11	4	1	100	25

Note: Total sample, 1989 inquiry: 75 Université Laval students.

[a]See table 1.5.

However, a third group, including both critical students and those with a positive attitude toward politics, was as sizable as the other groups. These students considered politics an important means to articulate their views and plans for society. They found wanting the current practice of politics but did not reject it per se. According to a 20-year-old male social services student: "I distinguish between politics as it should be and our day-to-day politics which does not function for the people but for the party, to keep one's job. We're moving away from the vision that politics is designed to represent and serve the people." He was not alone in expressing this view.

This distinction is certainly not new and is well known to all political commentators. Nevertheless, it is important to note that the distinction is not drawn as a theoretical tool for the detached commentator. Should we not view it as a sign, somewhat tenuous but nonetheless real, of the state of young people's reflection regarding the place of politics in our society and accordingly as a measure of their interest? And what if the view actually inhibited active participation in politics? A 23-year-old male business administration student responds: "Yes, of course [young people must take an interest in politics]. But you must make sure that you are not wasting your time. If you think you can't change the system, then you certainly won't change it. But even if I became involved, I don't think that would change anything."

If we look back in history, this view has a certain resonance. Gérard Pelletier, who had just joined the staff of Le Devoir as a journalist after several active years directing the Jeunesse étudiante catholique (JÉC) (Catholic Student Youth) movement, was already writing in a similar fashion in the 1940s:

> When we have clarified the issue of personal freedom vs. the party, when we have proved [to the current generation] that the tradition of inertia so closely linked with our partisan history is not necessarily the road all must follow, we shall have unleashed a huge force. But this act of liberation has not occurred. It has not even started. That is why so many young people are groping about, racked by fruitless anguish, grappling with diverse and contradictory impulses. (1948, 11)

Is this situation any different from today's? Whatever the conclusion, while the results of this first inquiry do force a more careful reading of the general critical assessment about young people's lack of political involvement, it does not support the rival claim that young people today share "a new conception of politics." The definitions and characterizations of politics found in our discussions with the students at the

Université Laval remain traditional. Yet a number of young people appear to be out of step with the practices of the contemporary political world; some, as a result, reject this world as a matter of principle.[9] Here, perhaps, can be derived an impression of "innovation and change." A more precise analysis, however, based on our interviews with these students suggests the more traditional interpretation.

A MEASURE OF POLITICAL INTEREST

The analysis of the results of the second inquiry with secondary school students provides new material to evaluate. This study, as noted earlier, is quite dissimilar to the one just considered: the group surveyed was at a different stage in the educational process, and information was not obtained through interviews but by questionnaire.[10] We will also compare the results of this survey with the results of others based on different samples of the population.

A Measured Interest

It was not surprising to learn that a majority of the secondary school students claimed that they were hardly or not at all interested in politics. Overall, some 40.7 percent of respondents in the 16–18 age group claimed to be either very or fairly interested in politics. Nonetheless, this minority figure is higher than the comparable result obtained in the Canadian Youth Foundation survey (1989) based on a representative sample of all young Canadians.[11]

A different reality can be discovered underneath this global figure. An analysis based on different sociological categories reveals different degrees of political interest. There is a significant divergence of opinion between young men and young women: roughly half the male secondary students declared a greater interest in politics, compared to one-third of the female students (table 1.7). Even though it was generally not high in absolute terms, the boys' more positive attitude was underscored by their relatively greater confidence in political parties (table 1.8). At the same time, girls who had studied mostly at private schools evinced more interest in politics than those with public school backgrounds; this distinction, however, does not apply to the boys (table 1.9).

The difference in attitude between boys and girls, and the difference among the girls is explained in part by the different socio-economic status of the young people surveyed (whether the father was a "senior manager" or a "blue-collar worker," for example).[12] However, certain results suggest that this background factor is not definitive. With girls in particular (see table 1.10), the public versus private school factor also influences the degree of interest in politics. Female students who have

Table 1.7
Stated interest in politics, by sex

	Very or fairly interested		Not very or not at all interested		Total	
	%	N	%	N	%	N
Male students	48.0	237	52.0	257	100	494
Female students	33.7	172	66.3	338	100	510
Total	40.7	409	59.3	595	100	1 004

Notes: Total sample = 1 008 secondary school students.
χ^2 = 21.1 (significant at 0.0001).

Table 1.8
Stated confidence in political parties, by sex

	Confident, on the whole		Not confident, on the whole		No response		Total	
	%	N	%	N	%	N	%	N
Male students	36.4	180	62.4	309	1.2	6	100	495
Female students	29.6	151	68.0	347	2.4	12	100	510
Total	32.9	331	65.3	656	1.8	18	100	1 005

Notes: Total sample = 1 008 secondary school students.
χ^2 = 6.5 (significant at 0.05).

Table 1.9
Stated interest in politics, according to private or public schooling, and by sex

	Very or fairly interested		Not very or not at all interested		Total	
	%	N	%	N	%	N
Male students						
Private	47.3	70	52.7	78	100	148
Public	48.3	166	51.7	178	100	344
Female students						
Private	50.8	62	49.2	60	100	122
Public	28.5	110	71.5	276	100	386
Total						
Private	48.9	132	51.1	138	100	270
Public	37.8	276	62.2	454	100	730

Notes: Total sample = 1 008 secondary school students.
χ^2 (male students) = 0.038 (significant at 0.90).
χ^2 (female students) = 20.6 (significant at 0.0001).

mainly attended public schools and whose fathers were categorized as "blue-collar" comprise the majority of young people with no interest in politics; the privately educated girls of similar backgrounds were less negative. Girls with fathers classified as "managers" also differed in their response toward politics depending on the nature of their schooling. There was a less marked divergence in this regard among boys whose fathers were in the blue-collar group, and the schooling factor was insignificant in explaining attitudes toward politics among sons of managers.

Table 1.10
Stated interest in politics, according to private or public schooling, by sex, and by father's occupation

	Very or fairly interested		Not very or not at all interested		Total*	
	%	N	%	N	%	N
Male students						
Private school						
Senior managers	49.1	28	50.9	29	100.0	57
Blue-collar workers	44.4	8	55.6	10	100.0	18
Public school						
Senior managers	55.1	49	45.0	40	100.1	89
Blue-collar workers	37.7	23	62.3	38	100.0	61
Female students						
Private school						
Senior managers	54.8	23	45.2	19	100.0	42
Blue-collar workers	55.6	5	44.4	4	100.0	9
Public school						
Senior managers	37.5	30	62.5	50	100.0	80
Blue-collar workers	23.7	22	76.3	71	100.0	93

Notes: Sample for this table = 452 secondary school students.

*Percentages may not add to 100.0 because of rounding.

Although these results must be interpreted with care – since the number of students surveyed who attended private schools and whose fathers were blue collar was not large enough to yield statistically significant results – private education does appear to stimulate interest in politics for students in general and for girls in particular.[13]

A large-scale study with follow-up interviews would permit further breakdowns and yield a sharper explanation of the observed differences. But such precision was not our objective. The importance here is to reveal through a narrow sampling of the "young" that interest in politics varies greatly among young people. In this context it is quite interesting to find that whereas three-quarters of girls who studied mainly in the public school sector indicated no interest in politics, more than half of the boys who attended public schools and whose fathers were managers claimed to be interested, or very interested, in politics.

It is certainly possible to go beyond a simple cross-tabulation of sociological variables to refine what is often an overly broad portrait of the degree of politicization of young people. Four other perspectives should be developed as interpretive guidelines. First of all, it is essential to place our survey results in context and to attempt some comparison with findings from previous studies. Second, our results should be reconciled with the picture drawn using other indicators of interest in politics. Third, it is necessary to determine whether the "rejection" of politics involves as well an aversion to all group activism. Finally, some distinction must be drawn between political activity and social involvement in the broad sense. On this point, we shall find that a large majority of young people participate in highly diverse groups.

It seems to us that a more complete picture of the nature and extent of young people's participation in community life can be drawn with the aid of these guidelines.

Four Observations on the Interpretation of Surveys on Political Interest

The Findings are Relative
The phenomenon of indifference toward politics is not confined to young people.[14] As Percheron (1987) has pointed out, the level of interest in politics among 15- to 24-year-olds in France never differs noticeably from that of the general population.[15] Politics in France generally has had a bad press and the abstention rate among adults during elections is high.[16]

If certain observers are expressing regrets that the behaviour of young people is no different from that of the older generation, perhaps those regrets arise from a notion of youth as the instrument of social change. But this image of youth, which became highly developed in certain writings of the 1960s, is only partially applicable and does not suggest adequate interpretations of inquiries such as our own.[17]

Even though sociological surveys were not as abundant as polemics at the end of the 1960s, certain facts do remind us of the real degree of young people's political concerns at the time. Consider, for example, the results of the 1964 study by Rioux and Sévigny (1965) which showed that over 70 percent of respondents ranked participation in associations, provincial politics and federal politics as their three lowest interests.[18] The phrasing of the question posed by the researchers may be disputed,[19] but this trend is confirmed by young people's expression – to a similar extent – of powerlessness to influence politics (Dumas et al. 1982, 43). It is also salutary to re-read the headlines in newspapers such as *Le Monde* during the spring of 1968, a period which has come to represent the essence of student militancy. Some journalists wrote at length of "student apathy and the decay of their organizations" and deplored that only a minority were truly committed. It is scarcely credible that they were writing within weeks of the "events."[20]

These examples are hardly given to minimize the influence of the student movement of the day; they illustrate that the assertion that young people were truly politicized in 1968 compared to today is a distortion of both history and contemporary reality. As Percheron (1987, 120) has observed, young people have always had their reservations about politics: "It is easy to mount evidence of young people's tentative attitudes about political parties and politicians: all studies on political socialization have underlined the early manifestation of such tendencies." Let us always bear in mind, particularly when analysing survey data about youth, that it is only a minority of young people (and adults, as well) who are truly active in politics.

Different Indicators of Political Interest

Any response to a question pertaining to an interest in politics must be ambiguous, since it is difficult to verify how the expression is understood. As a team of researchers headed by Suzanne Dumas found a few years ago: "Shouldn't students who follow major political events and exercise their right to vote be included among those who are designated to have a moderate interest in politics? Yet is this actually the case according to even the methods of political science?" (Dumas et al. 1982, 30).

An analysis of the other questions posed in the survey of high school students provides a better understanding of the nature of their interest in politics and certainly clarifies what young people understand by the term "political."

Concern over Political Decisions   The claim, advanced by many political scientists and sociologists, that an interest in politics is strongly linked to an individual's social integration[21] is simply the position that someone is not interested in politics because of general indifference to what is going on. A number of studies carried out in France in November and December 1986 in the wake of movements that were opposed to the proposed university reforms clearly showed that some young people took an interest because the question affected them personally. Until then, politics had apparently struck them as too abstract and remote.[22]

With this in mind, we asked the high school students if they felt personally concerned about the decisions then being made by government. Two aspects of their responses should be noted. First, the responses indicated a strong correlation between political interest and a feeling of concern regarding government decisions. Of the respondents who said they were very often or often concerned, 63 percent claimed to be very or fairly interested in politics, while of those who seldom or never felt concerned, only 17 percent were very or fairly interested. Second, and more strikingly, there were more students who said they were concerned than students who claimed to be interested in politics: 51.5 percent compared to 40.7 percent (compare tables 1.7 and 1.11). Here again, gender had strong statistical significance.

Such differences suggest that students distinguish between "the political game" (the image of politics that springs to mind when the term "politics" is mentioned) and "political actions" (decisions, measures that affect them in areas such as education, health, leisure). If so, any implication of true interest in politics would not be adequately captured through a measure of interest in "the political game."

Table 1.11
Concern about decisions made by government, by sex

	Very, or often concerned		Not very, or never concerned		Total	
	%	N	%	N	%	N
Male students	58.6	290	41.4	205	100	495
Female students	44.7	228	55.3	282	100	510
Total	51.5	518	48.5	487	100	1 005

Notes: Total sample = 1 008 secondary school students.
$\chi^2 = 19.4$ (significant at 0.0001).

Opinions about Political Institutions   The preceding hypothesis can be confirmed, in part, by examining other responses. The young people surveyed indicated that political parties and politicians are among the individuals and institutions they least trust. This is confirmed in other surveys, such as that published in *L'Actualité* (1989, 36), according to which two-thirds of young people had little or no confidence in politicians. The least esteemed, politicians, trailed far behind teachers, CEOs, and even journalists and trade unionists.[23] The survey of the Canadian Youth Foundation (1989, 37) showed that, among Canadians, young people in Quebec were the least inclined to be very, or fairly, confident in government leaders, whether federal, provincial or municipal, and the proportion of young people having confidence in each of these groups of leaders never exceeded 20 percent.

The only other group that received as low a confidence ranking as politicians was employers (table 1.12). This is of particular interest since 70 percent or more of the respondents claimed to trust businesses per se, along with banks, schools and the police.

Table 1.12
Expressed attitude of confidence, on the whole, in various institutions or individuals related to politics, by sex
(percentages)

	Male students	Female students	Total
Banks	88.1	92.2	90.2
Schools	79.4	87.5	83.5
Police	67.9	71.8	69.9
Business	68.9	70.4	69.7
Government	63.2	68.4	65.8
Church	58.2	63.9	61.1
Media	57.8	59.0	58.4
Justice system	56.2	55.7	56.0
Army	60.2	51.4	55.8
Labour unions	54.8	56.1	55.5
Elected representatives	39.4	41.6	40.5
Employers	42.6	35.1	38.9
Political parties	36.4	29.6	33.0

Note: Total sample = 1 008 secondary school students.

The level of confidence in elected representatives (table 1.12) seems to be unrelated to concerns over government decisions. In other words, as many young people who feel confident in elected members as those who do not may be concerned about political decisions (table 1.13).

By contrast, the same does not hold true for "interest in politics" (table 1.14), since more of the young people who say they have no confidence in elected representatives state that *they have no interest in politics.*

This difference between the results of tables 1.13 and 1.14 tends to show that some of the young people surveyed formed their negative image of politics and politicians based on "interest in politics," rather than on the idea of "feeling concerned about government decisions." Thus we cannot conclude, based on a single overall question about political interest, that young people reject (or do not reject) the entire realm of politics. A comparison of several indicators reveals that if a majority of young people reject politics, it is politics as it is practised, not politics as such.[24] It should be stressed, however, that the proportion of young

Table 1.13

Concern about decisions made by government, according to level of confidence in elected representatives

	Very, or often concerned		Not very, or never concerned		Total	
	%	N	%	N	%	N
Confident, on the whole	55.3	225	44.7	182	100	407
Not confident, on the whole	49.9	290	50.1	291	100	581

Notes: Sample for this table = 988 secondary school students.
$\chi^2 = 2.76$ (significant at 0.0964).

Table 1.14

Interest in politics, according to level of confidence in elected representatives

	Very or fairly interested		Not very or not at all interested		Total	
	%	N	%	N	%	N
Confident, on the whole	47.2	192	52.8	215	100	407
Not confident, on the whole	36.7	213	63.3	367	100	580

Notes: Sample for this table = 987 secondary school students.
$\chi^2 = 10.79$ (significant at 0.001).

people not concerned with politics does remain significant and that this interpretation does not apply to all young people; it is simply an additional consideration.

Further, although half the students interviewed at Université Laval believed that politics addressed important questions, they expressed serious reservations about the way in which politicians dealt with them (not necessarily because politicians acted in bad faith, but rather because of the cumbersome "machinery," the constraints, etc.). The following points raised by two students, the first a 23-year-old male in business administration studies, and the second a 21-year-old male political science student, illustrate this well:

> These questions are being taken care of, but in a rather cursory manner. It takes so much time. The machine is so big that before ideas and situations can be changed ... we have the impression that nothing is being done. The things that are being taken care of are the ones that people want, but not in a concrete fashion. There is a lot of talk but little action.

> At the level of "petty politics" of government, I think that serious debate on issues is being avoided. The issue of abortion has been tackled in a haphazard way and has been handed over to the Supreme Court. It almost seems that the government doesn't want to bother people with the issue, because either people are not interested or there's a lack of political will. That's petty management politics.

Responses to Open Partisanship   Further questions about their understanding of political parties (which, as noted, elicited a positive response from only one-third of those surveyed – table 1.12) are equally revealing. Two points of note are raised here as the last of the four indicators on our first question related to interest in politics.

One-quarter of high school students claim affiliation with a political party. Among those who do not, more than a third justify the situation on the grounds that they lack the necessary information. One-quarter who have no political affiliation are simply not interested, while the remainder qualify the situation by indicating that the current parties "do not reflect their ideas," or that they take their ideas from all of the existing parties.

There is clearly a relationship between the level of confidence in a political party and the fact of feeling close to it. It should, therefore, come as no surprise that nearly three-quarters of the young people who do not feel close to a party also state that they have no confidence in political parties. Nevertheless, some young people also indicate that although they have no confidence in political parties in general, they feel close to one of them. The relationship can therefore be more complex, with some young people sustaining a negative view of parties in general while at the same time not refusing to choose one, because they are, in effect, interested in politics generally. Throughout the entire survey, only a minority (11 percent) held this view. Yet it is interesting that nearly three-quarters of the respondents in this group state they are interested in politics, and that 83 percent often feel concerned by government decisions.

At the provincial level in Quebec, young people who feel close to a party lean more toward the Parti québécois than the Liberal Party of Quebec (72 percent would vote for the Parti québécois). At the federal level, responses are more divided. As table 1.15 indicates, a significant proportion of these young people did not respond when asked about parties at the federal level (12.8 percent), which is interesting when compared with the political choices made provincially.[25]

The Partisan Stance   For the entire sample, we were surprised to find that very few young people refused to indicate their preferences from a list of the major political parties, although the rate of non-response varied with the level of government.[26] Thus, only 9.4 percent of respondents did not respond when asked about their intention to vote at the provincial level (table 1.16), and 15 percent at the federal level (table 1.17). For the entire sample, young people in the Quebec City and Drummondville regions generally felt closer to the Parti québécois and, at the federal level, to the Progressive Conservative party.[27]

Table 1.15
Political party for which young people feel an affinity at the federal level, according to opinion about feeling close to a party in general

	PC		Liberal		NDP		Other		No response		Total	
	%	N	%	N	%	N	%	N	%	N	%	N
Yes, close to a party	42.4	103	29.2	71	11.5	28	4.1	10	12.8	31	100	243
No, not close to a party	41.7	319	33.9	259	6.1	47	2.2	17	16.1	123	100	765

Notes: Total sample = 1 008 secondary school students.
χ^2 = 12.20 (significant at 0.0159).

Table 1.16
Intention to vote at the provincial level, by sex
(percentages)

	PQ	LPQ	NDP	Other	No response	Total* %	N
Male students	55.8	29.5	1.6	4.6	8.5	100.0	495
Female students	52.4	29.6	1.2	6.7	10.2	100.1	510
Total	54.0	29.6	1.4	5.7	9.4	100.1	
(N)	(543)	(297)	(14)	(57)	(94)		(1 005)

Note: Total sample = 1 008 secondary school students.
*Percentage may not total 100.0 because of rounding.

Table 1.17
Intention to vote at the federal level, by sex
(percentages)

	PC	Liberal	NDP	Other	No response	Total* %	N
Male students	47.9	28.1	6.3	3.8	13.9	100.0	495
Female students	36.3	37.5	8.6	1.6	16.1	100.1	510
Total	42.0	32.8	7.5	2.7	15.0	100.0	
(N)	(422)	(330)	(75)	(27)	(151)		(1 005)

Note: Total sample = 1 008 secondary school students.
*Percentage may not total 100.0 because of rounding.

Although several other survey results could be explored, the four indicators of interest in politics just discussed suggest that young people are not as removed from the world of politics as one might think. In correlating our findings, we can state that only 38.5 percent of the young people surveyed claimed at the same time to have no interest in politics, to have no concern about political decisions and to feel no affinity to a party. We might call this finding a *general index of non-interest in politics*. Of this group, 60 percent are young women.

Interest in Social Action
Up to this point we have examined the record of the world of politics only in the narrow sense of political parties and politicians. This dimension is obviously insufficient to assess young people's interest in

politics. Political action encompasses much more than just political parties and large institutional structures. The willingness to undertake protest action against public authority is as indicative of young people's interest as is an expression of confidence in politicians and political parties. Signing petitions, writing to newspapers, joining a group or even standing for election – all comprise elements of what may be termed political interest.

A large majority of the students surveyed would agree to sign petitions or telephone people they know to defend an idea they believe in. However, this is hardly surprising given that this does not involve a particularly strong commitment.[28]

It is perhaps more surprising to note that one-third of the young people in the sample (table 1.18) would readily agree to write to newspapers or to a politician, or even to belong to a group or association (38 percent). One-quarter would agree to stand for election.[29] If we add to these percentages the respondents who would "perhaps" agree to such activity,[30] we find that at least half of the young people would agree to undertake these initiatives.

Contrary to our earlier findings, few gender differences were observed and, where these existed, they tended to show a greater "availability" on the part of young women (except for boycotting products). For example, more female students than males indicated they would be prepared to join a group to defend an idea they believe in (table 1.19). Yet, have the young women not claimed to be less interested in politics?

Table 1.18
Participation in a series of activities to defend a cause, by sex
(percentages)

	Male students	Female students	Total
Sign petitions	69.5	77.7	73.6
Telephone people you know	55.8	62.4	59.1
Join a group	37.4	39.8	38.6
Write to a politician	32.3	33.9	33.1
Write to a newspaper	31.5	31.8	31.7
Demonstrate in the street	33.9	26.7	30.3
Boycott products	35.6	22.0	28.8
Stand for election to a responsible position	25.9	24.9	25.4
Hold a sit-in in an office	19.2	17.8	18.5

Note: Total sample = 1 008 secondary school students.

Table 1.19
Participation in a group or association to defend a cause, by sex

	Yes, certainly		Yes, perhaps		No, not really		No		Total*	
	%	N	%	N	%	N	%	N	%	N
Male students	37.7	185	37.9	186	17.5	86	6.9	34	100.0	491
Female students	39.8	203	42.4	216	13.9	71	3.9	20	100.0	510
Total	38.8	388	40.1	402	15.7	157	5.4	54	100.1	1 001

Notes: Total sample = 1 008 secondary school students.
$\chi^2 = 7.8$ (significant at 0.01).
*Percentage may not total 100.0 because of rounding.

One-third of the young people surveyed, according to the most conservative estimate, would be ready to make a firm "commitment." Further, the responses to this question do not necessarily depend on questions that have been studied up to now – which tends to establish, in our opinion, that among young people there is little connection between the perception of the "political game" and that of political actions.

At least one-third of the young people who said they felt little or no interest in politics would readily participate in the lobbying activities proposed in the survey to defend an idea they believe in. It is only in refining the indicators further and in using, for example, the general index of interest in politics (which, it will be remembered, takes into account both a negative interest in politics and a feeling of no political allegiance) that the number of young people who would readily agree to such activity declines significantly (table 1.20).

Admittedly, this indicates only a potential attitude toward participation. The survey conducted by the Canadian Youth Foundation (1989, 37) completes the preceding data. Forty percent of those surveyed have signed a petition while only 18 percent have participated in a demonstration, 13 percent have written to an "official"[31] and 8 percent have boycotted products in stores. A comparison of these figures with those in table 1.18 reveals a gap between the expression of commitment and its actual fulfilment.[32] Still, the figures reveal an interesting potential: with the signing of petitions and telephoning friends excluded, only 35.2 percent said they had never felt willing to undertake some "political" action. This figure belies a clear rejection of political action (and therefore of politics) on the part of young people.

Table 1.20
Participation in a series of activities to defend a cause, according to the general index of interest in politics
(percentages)

	Interested	Not interested	Aggregate[a]
Sign petitions	83.5	66.3	73.7
Telephone people you know	65.9	55.1	59.1
Join a group	61.2	22.6	38.1
Write to a politician	59.4	19.3	33.1
Write to a newspaper	52.4	19.3	31.6
Demonstrate in the street	53.5	16.5	30.3
Boycott products	54.1	14.1	28.7
Stand for election to a responsible position	42.9	13.9	25.4
Hold a sit-in in an office	31.2	9.3	18.5

Notes: Total sample = 1 008 secondary school students.

[a]The percentage included under "Aggregate" is not an average of "Interested" and "Not interested," since these two indices are the extremes. (Young people replying negatively to one of the three index components are excluded. The number of respondents grouped under the two indices is 559.)

Participation

The fact that 43 percent of the students surveyed who felt little or no interest in politics responded they would defend an idea they believed in or join a group or association points to an interesting reality. The social participation of young people should be integrated with an analysis of the politicization of youth, since it is a component of the problem that arises in comments about youth. As we emphasized in the first part of this study, young people are supposed to be not only *apolitical* – a notion which we have attempted to clarify – but also individualists who refuse to participate in organized activities. However, participation in the social life of a community is not necessarily linked to an interest in politics – a fortiori when it is the politics of politicians. The link between "rejection of politics" and "individualism" is not obvious; in fact, our results tend to suggest that the opposite is the case.

In fact, a significant proportion (some two-thirds) of grade 11 and 12 students surveyed stated that they participated in at least one kind of group activity, whether it be sports, cultural, school-related or other. Most of them had been participating for some time: nearly one-half for more than two years; only 14 percent for less than six months. A little less than a third set aside one or two hours a week, but the others indicated they spent several hours and even part of the weekend on these activities.

Contrary to what is sometimes claimed, part-time work, which is becoming more and more important for young people of this age,[33] is not a determining factor in the rate of participation. In fact, as table 1.21 shows, over one-third of those surveyed who belonged to only one group or association also worked part time. This proportion is lower than that of those who did not participate at all, but it is also lower compared with that of those who participated in two or even three organizations. It is hard to conclude that working part time hinders participation.

It is true, of course, that this first *overall participation index* conceals a number of realities. If we classify these, for the purposes of this study, into seven types of groups (we shall call them "organizations"), we can see that the *effective* participation percentages vary from one to the other (table 1.22).

A majority of the young people surveyed participated first and foremost in sports groups, followed by groups of a cultural nature (theatre, music and dance groups, improvisation leagues and so on). In looking at the strictly political organizations (political parties and their youth wings) and those with political objectives (humanitarian organizations, human rights associations and ecological movements), we see that the latter attract more members than the former, although they attracted scarcely 10 percent of the young people surveyed. Thus, of the roughly 1 000 young people surveyed, only 45 belonged to a humanitarian association and 24 belonged to a political organization.

Table 1.21
Participation in a group or organization, in relation to part-time employment

	Participates		Does not participate		Total	
	%	N	%	N	%	N
Does not work	54.8	228	45.2	188	100	416
Works less than 15 hours a week	65.4	240	34.6	127	100	367
Works more than 15 hours a week	67.6	150	32.4	72	100	222
Total	61.5	618	38.5	387	100	1 005

Notes: Total sample = 1 008 secondary school students.
$\chi^2 = 13.7$ (significant at .0011).

Table 1.22
Participation in a group or organization
(percentages)

	Participates	Has already participated	Would like to participate	Would not like to participate	Total* %	Total* N
Organizations with political objectives						
Male students	10.9	9.5	70.5	9.1	100.0	495
Female students	6.1	7.5	81.4	5.0	100.0	510
Total	8.5	8.5	76.0	7.0	100.0	
(N)	(85)	(85)	(764)	(71)		(1 005)
Organizations with cultural objectives						
Male students	27.0	16.0	38.0	19.0	100.0	495
Female students	30.0	35.3	31.0	3.7	100.0	510
Total	28.6	25.8	34.4	11.2	100.0	
(N)	(287)	(259)	(346)	(113)		(1 005)
Organizations with leisure-time objectives						
Male students	8.5	12.5	37.2	41.8	100.0	495
Female students	5.9	9.8	42.9	41.4	100.0	510
Total	7.2	11.1	40.1	41.6	100.0	
(N)	(72)	(112)	(403)	(418)		(1 005)
Organizations with socialization objectives (army cadets, Scouts, religious movements)						
Male students	14.3	32.3	31.5	21.9	100.0	495
Female students	12.4	38.2	23.1	26.3	100.0	510
Total	13.3	35.3	27.3	24.1	100.0	
(N)	(134)	(355)	(274)	(242)		(1 005)
Sports organizations						
Male students	41.6	31.3	20.8	6.3	100.0	495
Female students	22.8	31.0	31.0	15.3	100.1	510
Total	32.2	31.1	25.9	10.8	100.0	
(N)	(322)	(313)	(261)	(109)		(1 005)
Political organizations per se						
Male students	3.0	1.6	33.1	62.3	100.0	495
Female students	1.8	0.8	26.5	70.9	100.0	510
Total	2.4	1.2	29.8	66.6	100.0	
(N)	(24)	(12)	(299)	(670)		(1 005)
School-related organizations						
Male students	9.9	19.6	39.8	30.7	100.0	495
Female students	13.7	21.4	41.6	23.3	100.0	510
Total	11.8	20.5	40.7	27.0	100.0	
(N)	(119)	(206)	(409)	(271)		(1 005)

Note: Total sample = 1 008 secondary school students.

*Percentage may not total 100.0 because of rounding.

While these figures are small, they are similar to findings in the studies cited earlier.[34]

Although groups with a political objective did not attract high participation, the interviewers indicated that they did foster stronger allegiance than did political parties themselves. This was especially striking during our first survey among Université Laval students. Many respondents did not hesitate to reject political parties in favour of humanitarian associations; for example, this 23-year-old male accounting student, when asked what organization struck him as noteworthy, responded:

> Certainly not the political parties. If I were to get involved in something, it would be in an environmental pressure group. Aside from that, I think it's a waste of time. Political parties are fine for a time, but after that, you get fed up ... Once they've done their funny business, then they reward their friends.

A 23-year-old female anthropology student also spoke out strongly for humanitarian organizations:

> The United Appeal, the Red Cross, and disarmament and peace organizations are important because they provide information and increase awareness. Without them, people wouldn't give a damn about these problems.

However, this expressed interest does not actually result in broader commitment. This fact is rarely stressed, although it has been apparent for some years. As noted by one commentator (Bélanger 1986, 52) during a 1985 symposium on the place of young people in Quebec politics:

> It seems very clear that the drop in participation and militancy among young people in those organizations in which they used to be very active (political parties and student associations) has not been offset by higher participation in other groups and, in particular, in organizations working specifically in their interests, such as ecological and pacifist groups, and youth groups.

That the participation rates are low when broken down into each type of group activity does not mean an outright rejection of the groups by the other young people surveyed. Of these, the proportion *who did not wish to participate at all* remains rather low. Only the strictly political organizations fared badly (two-thirds would refuse to participate – a slightly higher percentage among female students, as seen in table 1.22).

If we exclude the overall participation index for sports groups, cultural groups and leisure-time groups to form a limited participation index, the rate of participation is slightly higher than one student in four, which is by no means marginal (table 1.23).

It appears very important to us to separate a nucleus of young participants in this manner, even if the organizations in which they participate are not always political in the strict sense of the term. The actual socialization process through these organizations will not necessarily be "political" but it can contribute to the development of a certain political interest, according to the terminology that we have gradually been developing throughout this study. Moreover, as table 1.24 shows, those who took part in a group or an association (excluding sports, cultural and leisure-time organizations) were divided about their interest in politics, but were less so when it came to their concerns about government decisions (table 1.25).

An examination of other periods in history shows that there were sometimes organizations, hardly termed "political," that prepared future leaders for public life in politics and in other social leadership roles. The Catholic Action movements of the 1940s, for example, were the training ground for many political leaders.[35] These movements nonetheless rejected politics as it was practised at the time, at least as it pertained to French Canada. The JÉC movement never advocated participation in traditional politics but rather an ongoing commitment to the student community. However, the foremost leaders of the time developed a feeling for the world around them that guided them for the rest of their lives. As Pelletier wrote (1985, quoted in Fournier 1989) in honouring the fiftieth anniversary of an organization of which he was one of the

Table 1.23
Participation in a group (with the exception of sports, cultural or leisure-time groups – limited participation index), by sex

	Participates		Has already participated		Would like to participate		Would not like to participate		Total*	
	%	N	%	N	%	N	%	N	%	N
Male students	27.9	138	36.2	179	32.8	162	3.0	15	100	494
Female students	26.7	136	39.1	199	33.4	170	0.8	4	100	509
Total	27.3	274	37.7	378	33.1	332	1.9	19	100	1 003

Note: Total sample = 1 008 secondary school students.

*Percentage may not total 100.0 because of rounding.

Table 1.24
Stated interest in politics, according to limited participation index (table 1.23)

	Very or quite interested		Fairly, or not at all interested		Total	
	%	N	%	N	%	N
Participates	51.6	142	48.4	133	100	275
Has already participated	41.3	157	58.7	223	100	380
Would like to participate	32.9	109	67.1	222	100	331
Would not like to participate	10.5	2	89.5	17	100	19

Notes: Total sample = 1 008 secondary school students.
χ^2 = 29.2 (significant at 0.0001).

Table 1.25
Concern about decisions made by government, according to limited participation index (table 1.23)

	Very often, or often concerned		Hardly, or never concerned		Total	
	%	N	%	N	%	N
Participates	61.5	169	38.5	106	100.0	275
Has already participated	50.0	190	50.0	190	100.0	380
Would like to participate	46.7	155	53.3	177	100.0	332
Would not like to participate	26.3	5	73.7	14	100.0	19

Notes: Total sample = 1 008 secondary school students.
χ^2 = 19.2 (significant at 0.0007).

main leaders from 1939 to 1944: "Membership in this movement, its irruption into our adolescence, constituted for hundreds of women and men of my generation a spiritual experience and an extremely significant apprenticeship in social action."

Today there are no movements to equal the JÉC, either in kind or in strength of influence. Today, socialization takes on other forms and draws young people in different directions.

Without specifically identifying this participation as a form of politicization, it is necessary to underscore that a majority of young people have not abandoned groups and group activities. Further, this participation is a significant source of socialization and development of an interest in the public sphere. Other data will have to be added subsequently to clarify how young people are socialized today by such groups. It is these young people who will take over, as a 22-year-old male political science student at Université Laval noted during the interviews we conducted in 1989:

> We are the future. Brian [Mulroney] is there, but in 30 years he will no longer be there. It is important to take over economically, socially ... The baby boom is now in its final phase. Some of us are going to take over. This will be done quietly. The USSR is cleaning house; we'll have to do as much at some point, too. Young people are paying closer attention to politics, even though they are not getting involved, but it does affect them directly. If I'm not mistaken, things will get better. The upcoming generation will be better educated than the people in power now, they will be better trained; we'll be able to tackle problems more quickly.

AGENDA FOR ACTION

Based on the thesis that we have attempted to clarify and develop, one constant persists: young people acquire an interest in politics or the world of public affairs through an indirect process, one which results from socialization, apprenticeship in the broadest sense of the term, discussions with parents and friends, the desire to follow through on a commitment shared with peers, reading newspapers and so on.[36] An interest in politics never "just develops" nor is it sustained by one particular age group.

Thus, we believe that there are measures that can be taken to encourage a greater politicization of young people. Yet it is necessary to keep in mind that these are limited and that they are not a panacea for a situation which, it must be kept in mind, is not necessarily perceived as a "problem" by those affected. Our study therefore cannot recommend a specific reform, the creation of new organizations or the adoption of a targeted policy suggesting the way to change the present situation in a radical manner. That would be as useful as slicing water with a knife!

However, the Royal Commission on Electoral Reform and Party Financing could send a message that the value of public life should be enhanced. In particular, the Commission could encourage:

- a debate on lowering the voting age to 16;
- participation in group activities;
- the creation of courses to introduce students to political life.

The Right to Vote at 16

Are young people today in favour of lowering the voting age? As a number of them claim to be interested in politics and at the same time dissatisfied with what is now happening on the political scene, would they not be in favour of this measure?

In a recent paper, two Canadian researchers (Bibby and Posterski 1985, 5) quoted the remarks of a young male Newfoundland student, very likely under the age of 18. The student claimed that older people prevented young people from becoming adults. His argument ran as follows:

> I wish teenagers' opinions were taken more seriously, especially on political matters. Like females a hundred years ago, we are a minority group. Maybe in a hundred years' time, teens will have the right to vote and other rights.

However, there is an absence of consensus even among young people concerning the idea of lowering the voting age, regardless of the minimum age selected. Disagreement can be found, no matter what the social milieu of the young people. In 1989, in interviews for another study involving 15- to 20-year-old French young people, a number of respondents were highly reserved about this issue, even in the restricted case of more active student participation in political organizations:

> It would be a good idea to lower the voting age. Well, it could be a bad thing, too, because at 16 one is more impressionable. Not everybody has made a choice. However, my mind is made up ... I can't wait to vote, but lowering the voting age would be risky. Voting must be personal and not influenced by anyone.

Many respondents were frankly hostile to lowering the voting age: "No, no, no ... We must be given the time to mature, gain experience, listen, read and see. At 16, we are still influenced by our parents and friends."

One question from our 1990 survey of students from grades 11 and 12 from the Quebec City and Drummondville regions was designed to ascertain whether the voting age should be lowered to 16. Our findings are unambiguous: 40 percent of the respondents were in favour of such a measure, while a majority opposed it (table 1.26). Yet surprisingly, two-thirds of the same young people believed that the right to vote is one of the best ways of "ensuring that politics reflects their ideas."[37]

Table 1.26
Opinions on the right to vote at age 16, by sex

	In agreement		Not in agreement		No response[a]		Total	
	%	N	%	N	%	N	%	N
Male students	45.7	226	52.1	258	2.2	11	100	495
Female students	37.6	192	61.2	312	1.2	6	100	510
Total	41.6	418	56.7	570	1.7	17	100	1 005

Notes: Total sample = 1 008 secondary school students.

χ^2 (excluding "no response") = 7.5 (significant at 0.01).

[a]As the "no response" figure was increased very little by this question, it will be omitted from subsequent tables.

Those who express this opinion do not, however, alter their views on the right to vote at age 16. Only one-third of those in complete agreement that having the vote is necessary for politics to reflect their ideas would grant the right to vote to 16-year-olds. Thus the two variables seem to be independent: the vote is the means to an end but this does not in itself justify granting it to those under 18.

We propose in what follows to examine the issue more closely as we did for the general question of interest in politics. As in the latter case, there were significant differences of opinion between male and female students: the former were more in favour of lowering the voting age than the latter (table 1.26).

Unlike the issue of interest in politics, age was a determining factor (table 1.27); the younger the respondents, the more they were in favour of lowering the voting age to 16: 46.1 percent of respondents 16 and under supported the measure. This figure falls to 37.8 percent among 18-year-olds. The crossing of the two variables (age and sex) does not alter this trend: age played an important role in the responses of students of both sexes (table 1.28).

It is difficult to interpret this trend with certainty. In terms of value judgements, the results indicate that the youngest people surveyed were more "permissive" than the oldest. Does this also affect responses to the voting question? Or, from another viewpoint, is it that 18-year-olds do not want to see a right they have just attained granted to younger people?[38] From our data it is hard to answer this question without specifically querying young people on that point. However, the difference is there – and it is significant.

Table 1.27
Opinions on the right to vote at age 16, by age

	In agreement		Not in agreement		Total	
	%	N	%	N	%	N
Age 16 and under	46.1	124	53.9	145	100	269
Age 17	43.3	213	56.7	279	100	492
Age 18	37.8	71	62.2	117	100	188
Age 19 and over	22.9	8	77.1	27	100	35
Total	42.3	416	57.7	568	100	984

Notes: Total sample = 1 008 secondary school students.
$\chi^2 = 8.8$ (significant at 0.05).

Table 1.28
Opinions on the right to vote at age 16, according to sex and age

	In agreement		Not in agreement		Total*	
	%	N	%	N	%	N
Male students						
Age 16 and under	50.8	67	49.2	65	100.0	132
Age 17	48.0	120	52.0	130	100.0	250
Age 18	38.6	32	61.4	51	100.0	83
Age 19 and over	31.3	5	68.8	11	100.1	16
Total	46.6	224	53.4	257	100.0	481
Female students						
Age 16 and under	41.6	57	58.4	80	100.0	137
Age 17	38.4	93	61.6	149	100.0	242
Age 18	37.1	39	62.9	66	100.0	105
Age 19 and over	15.8	3	84.2	16	100.0	19
Total	38.2	192	61.8	311	100.0	503

Note: Total sample = 1 008 secondary school students.
*Percentage may not total 100.0 because of rounding.

Overall, it should be noted that the fact of feeling very, or somewhat interested in politics influenced opinion on the right to vote. Table 1.29 shows that those who were very, or somewhat interested were more in favour of lowering the voting age to 16, though the gap is not always significant (the same holds true for differences according to sex – table 1.30).

Moreover, the differences are also of slight significance when opinions on the right to vote are compared with the feeling of being concerned about political decisions. Forty-five percent of those who admitted concern would agree to see the political age of majority lowered to 16, while 60 percent of those who rarely felt concerned did not agree with such a measure.

Even among those young people who participated in groups other than those with sports, cultural or leisure-time focus, the majority did not favour the right to vote at age 16 (table 1.31). Four out of 10 young people who participate in such groups would agree. The correlation of

Table 1.29
Opinions on the right to vote at age 16, according to age and stated interest in politics

	In agreement		Not in agreement		Total	
	%	N	%	N	%	N
Age 16 and under						
Very, or quite interested	47.6	50	52.4	55	100	105
Not very, or not at all interested	45.1	74	54.9	90	100	164
Total	46.1	124	53.9	145	100	269
Age 17						
Very, or quite interested	48.8	98	51.2	103	100	201
Not very, or not at all interested	39.3	114	60.7	176	100	290
Total	43.2	212	56.8	279	100	491
Age 18						
Very, or quite interested	34.6	27	65.4	51	100	78
Not very, or not at all interested	40.0	44	60.0	66	100	110
Total	37.8	71	62.2	117	100	188
Age 19						
Very, or quite interested	28.6	4	71.4	10	100	14
Not very, or not at all interested	19.0	4	81.0	17	100	21
Total	22.9	8	77.1	27	100	35

Note: Sample for this table = 983 secondary school students.

Table 1.30
Opinions on the right to vote at age 16, according to sex and stated interest in politics

	In agreement		Not in agreement		Total	
	%	N	%	N	%	N
Male students						
Very, or quite interested	48.7	112	51.3	118	100	230
Not very, or not interested	44.7	113	55.3	140	100	253
Total	46.6	225	53.4	258	100	483
Female students						
Very, or quite interested	40.0	68	60.0	102	100	170
Not very, or not interested	37.1	124	62.9	210	100	334
Total	38.1	192	61.9	312	100	504

Note: Total sample = 1 008 secondary school students.

Table 1.31
Opinions on the right to vote at age 16, according to limited participation index (table 1.23)

	In agreement		Not in agreement		Total*	
	%	N	%	N	%	N
Participates	43.8	119	56.3	153	100.1	272
Has already participated	42.8	158	57.1	221	99.9	379
Would like to participate	40.5	132	59.5	194	100.0	326
Would not like to participate	47.4	9	52.6	10	100.0	19
Total	42.3	418	57.7	570	100.0	988

Notes: Total sample = 1 008 secondary school students.
$\chi^2 = 2.4$ (significant at 0.66).
*Percentage may not total 100.0 because of rounding.

the question of lowering the voting age with certain types of group activity reveals some interesting differences. More than half (54.8 percent) of the young people who participated in groups with political objectives (humanitarian associations, ecological movements and so on – excluding political parties per se) would agree to a lowering of the voting age, but only 38.7 percent of those who were involved with student newspapers or radio would be in favour of the measure. Except in certain associations, where the students appeared to have considered the question, few results permit us to conclude that there is a majority interest in lowering the voting age.

Why, then, propose such a measure?

An examination of surveys, particularly those carried out in France when the voting age was lowered from 21 to 18 (in 1974), shows that a significant proportion of young people were overtly opposed to the measure at the time. Yet, today, no one would question this decision. On the contrary, it is clear that a significant number of young people in certain "categories" (males and the youngest, on whom such a measure could have a psychological impact)[39] would welcome it. It is perhaps here that we come to the nub of one of the main hypotheses of this study: the search, based on surveys, for a *majority* opinion that has little chance of emerging can lead us to neglect realities that are no less important.

In our opinion, the proposal to lower the voting age would doubtless lead to a debate on the role of politics in our society. Moreover, at a time when many legal rights are granted at the age of 16 (e.g., the right to drive, the age at which one can legally leave school), why should young people be subject to a few more years' delay in political matters?

An analysis of the parliamentary debate on the age of majority and political eligibility in France clearly indicates that the question of lowering or raising the voting age is a totally arbitrary one, without a rigorous logical foundation (Fournier and Pépratx 1991). In some cases, the question is simply one of conforming with provisions in other legislation on the age of majority (e.g., the Civil Code) while, in others, the right must be withdrawn "to protect the country from the excesses of its young people." In other words, such a decision is truly an act of political will.

Encourage Participation in Community Activities

French surveys on this issue clearly indicate that young people vote less than the population at large. It does not necessarily follow that lowering the voting age will automatically arouse an interest in politics, although it does strike us as much more important, in addition, to encourage political education measures in the broad sense of the term. Such initiatives could prove not only extremely useful, but also necessary, in demonstrating that an extension of the franchise is eminently sensible. One such possibility is to propose introductory political life courses in secondary schools, a proposal to which we shall return later.

Similarly, we could encourage young people to engage in extracurricular activities in conjunction with their school programs.[40] Whatever else is done, interventionist and authoritarian measures in this area are not advisable. Above all, it must be kept in mind that socialization is not a one-way process: individuals transform social structures as much as they are transformed by them. And that is equally true when it comes to social integration.

The few historic allusions in this study show clearly that the relationship with politics cannot adequately be depicted solely by considering personal testimonials or by specific analysis of first-hand observations of political life. As the views of some of the students in our study have made clear, politics can thrive, and thrive effectively, even while we are not fully conscious of it.

Within the framework of the present Commission's work, and even despite the nature of its mandate, it is relevant to recall that the pursuit of the democratic ideal does not hinge solely on the rules and conditions of partisan political machines or organizations. The role and function of such organizations are obviously essential. It is striking, however, that the democratic function of political parties seems to have been better realized when a multiplicity of other diverse groups and organizations have contested the right of the established parties to represent the "popular will," or have at least called into question the legitimacy of any pretension to a monopoly on representing the interests of the people.

For electoral democracy to attain its true significance, on the one hand, and so that it is not undermined by the defeat of its current political organizations, on the other, it may be useful to enlarge the concept of democratic life. By defining democracy in terms that encompass the broadest possible meaning of "politics" and by drawing new horizons beyond those of political parties and parliamentary institutions, perhaps we can develop more positive perceptions of collective action and even revive the impulse to group commitment. The results of our inquiries indicate quite clearly that young people have not given up on group projects. Although many of them are losing hope in this regard, even when provided with the necessary tools, it is also evident that certain institutional mechanisms at their disposal do not appear very inviting. But must the picture be so bleak?

If we return to the histories of political leaders, past and present, it becomes apparent that partisan political life was not their only route to social effectiveness. The "schools" of student associations, leisure-time groups, sports clubs, Catholic Action movements and so on contributed greatly to developing the commitment and skills that a number of them would, one day, apply in the political arena.

The Rehabilitation of Politics

Politics is essentially self-directed community activity. Unfortunately, politics needs to improve its community image. Politics is criticized as obscure and foreign partly because its complexity cannot be grasped. At almost every opportunity it is reviled as the source of the world's worst despotisms, if only to obscure one's disappointment with its more mundane failings and its daily activity. And it is condemned, eagerly and virulently, for every deviation from society's rules of ethics – perhaps with the main result of underscoring the fragility of the virtuous will of the people.

But let us be clear. Politics cannot indulge in the luxury of putting itself above all morality, especially not in its present state of health! We must, however, remind ourselves that politics as it is pursued does not necessarily correspond with politics as ideally conceived. Several other human pursuits would also be condemned without appeal if society imposed the same requirements as it imposes on people who follow a political career. Without yielding to a cynicism which has already afflicted the minds of too many citizens or without adopting an overly tolerant attitude that would produce even more perverse and negative effects, we must find means of perceiving and conceiving politics for what it is and what it can be.

An early apprenticeship to social life within an organized group is certainly an effective means to this end. Moreover, we could perhaps imagine that actual educational apprenticeship in political life, which would come in the last year of secondary school, would contribute to development of the democratic spirit. We do not have in mind the instruction of politics from a single theoretical point of view or from a narrow institutional perspective; we would then risk producing more dropouts than citizens committed to the advantages of participatory democracy. We are thinking more along the lines of the Quebec grade 12 secondary school course, *Introduction to Economic Life*, where the students simulate a stock exchange and discuss current economics, before turning to the mastery of supply-and-demand curves and becoming specialists in the law of declining trends in the profit rate!

Could it then be argued, however, that such an approach would impede the training of scientists, engineers and technicians? But can economic and technical progress, in itself, really obscure a collective vision of society? Can this discussion, in fact, be credible in these times when individualism and private enterprise apparently take pride of place? The young people who responded to our inquiry did not seem to be so self-absorbed – an attitude that has often been attributed to young people without sufficient analysis. At the very least we should remind ourselves that all young people will be called upon to exercise the role of citizens with all its attendant powers and responsibilities.

Clearly, it would be too simplistic to reduce the whole question of interest in politics and participation in political life to that of the right to vote. We have tried instead to show how these matters are linked and how they can influence each other. Doubtless, this debate removed from the academic to the public forum could lead to a whole series of explicit discussions on our society's criteria for participation in political life as well as an implicit review of citizens' interest in their political system. One could then add to the discussion the views on politics of the young people in our inquiry. And perhaps they then would feel somewhat more assured, if we deigned to listen to them, that there is more to life than merely looking out for oneself.

CONCLUSION

As we indicated at the outset, a multidimensional and occasionally contradictory portrait has emerged from our study of the opinions of young people regarding politics. It is impossible to portray youth unequivocally and unambiguously. To claim that young people do some things and do not do others says very little, except for those seeking to define by way of slogans or headlines. To speak about politicized youth without being more specific, without reservation or without clarification, is at base quite meaningless.

The actual comments of students have clearly shown that young people today draw a distinction between their perception of politics and their conception of what it ought to be. This study has established that the level of interest in politics will vary according to the type of questions used and the analysis that is made, the "reference point," as we termed it in the introduction.

It may be useful to recall our main indicators of political interest and the general results we have noted:

- *General index of interest in politics:* 61.5 percent of secondary school students surveyed said they were interested in politics, or were concerned about political decisions or still felt an affiliation for a political party.
- *Indication of partisan preference:* only 10 percent of the students surveyed refused to indicate a preference for a political party at the provincial level (majority preference, Parti québécois); 15 percent at the federal level (majority preference, Progressive Conservative party).

- *Inclination toward community action:* in reference to a specific type of action (joining a group, writing to the newspapers, participating in demonstrations, etc.), 64.8 percent of the students surveyed felt that they would not hesitate to use, at least once, one of these avenues to defend an idea they believed in.
- *General participation index:* 61.5 percent of students surveyed said they participated in a group, an association, a club or an organization of some kind.
- *Limited participation index:* 27.3 percent of students surveyed said they belonged to a group other than a sports, cultural or leisure-time group.
- *Right to vote at age 16:* 41.5 percent of students surveyed would agree to lowering the voting age to 16.

The reason for presenting our results according to these different indices is not to show that the 50 percent interest threshold has been surpassed and to thereby conclude that "young people are politicized." Rather, we've presented the responses in this manner to show that a regrouping of *questions* can alter the interpretation of young people's conception of "politics." Two comments are relevant.

First, in our opinion, there are still young people today who participate, or wish to participate, in "political activities." They may more often be members of humanitarian associations or ecological movements than of political parties; whatever their activity, such groups will help them feel involved and can stimulate a taste for commitment, political or otherwise. Other young people join student newspapers, the Scouts or religious movements. Sports clubs, too, contribute to individual development as well as team spirit; they foster a respect for competition *and* for play.[41]

Samples drawn on the entire youth population sometimes prevent us from grasping this reality. The number of young people who participate may even appear negligible (see table 1.22 on participation by type of group); we must keep in mind that the reality of participation, of interest in politics, remains nearly always a *minority phenomenon*. If all of today's young people are not interested in politics, *all* of them never have been, even during the most widespread mobilizations. Rezsohazy (1983, 97), for example, rightly points out that the actual proportion of young people, in the broad sense of the term, who were actively committed, even during the greatest upheavals on U.S. campuses, never exceeded 10 percent. "Politicization," the taste for personal commitment, remains a minority phenomenon within a population as a whole, whether it be young people or adults, so long as society is not going through a severe crisis state.

It remains to be seen whether the modes of political socialization offered by contemporary groups will bring forth results as remarkable as those produced by, among others, Quebec's Catholic Action movements of the 1940s. It is, nevertheless, regrettable that the young people who are active in groups do not attract more attention. Do they deliberately seek to stay in the background? The problem is not related to communication or the media. Today, these young people appear to be undertaking what is, by and large, a solitary initiative that is little remarked and that is performed apart from both their peers and society at large. If we examine the comments of students, it is readily apparent that most young people who participate do not feel that they are in any way acting on behalf of their contemporaries. This does not mean that they never participate with a view to helping others, but that they simply do it on their own behalf. To some extent, it may be said that the young people surveyed do not feel part of a group, whether it be a particular generation or any other minority that would move them to declare themselves or act publicly on its behalf. The concept of "militant youth" no longer exists.

Some young people deplore this fact of life. As evidence, one need only read interviews with French students in the wake of the November–December 1986 demonstrations. This one-time event enabled them to feel truly committed and to believe that everyone present, as a group, was defending the same goals and a common cause:

> For three weeks we were at the centre of everything, we were intensely, completely involved. I had a feeling of power. We were one million, shoulder to shoulder, in the streets. We met a lot of people and felt united. [Beforehand] we had the impression that nothing would ever happen. The movement revealed possibilities; [it proved that] young people shared certain values. Across the diverging opinions (from the moderate Right to the far Left), divisions were overcome. (Hudon and Lecomte 1987, 30, 31)

In our view, this is far removed from what other young people have experienced under different circumstances. It is in this spirit that we are frankly biased in the debate on lowering the voting age to 16. We cannot urge strongly enough that young people's participation in group activities be explicitly recognized and practically encouraged. Such a contribution from the adult world, which cannot evade its responsibility for the socialization of generations yet to come, would be particularly worthwhile and effective.

APPENDIX

The 1989 Inquiry

This initial inquiry focused on young university students' opinions about politics. The 75 respondents were selected in two stages according to certain basic criteria.[42]

The sample thus obtained does not claim to be representative of the population of Université Laval, of Quebec universities overall, or even less of young people in Quebec in general. Political science students were deliberately given a more important place in the survey, since the subject under study was particularly relevant to them. Because the objective of the study was to collect a range of opinions rather than to establish statistically significant percentages, we chose this method as the most promising.[43]

The same two people conducted all the interviews, according to standard research procedure, using a grid of general questions tested through an exploratory survey. The interviews were conducted between November 1988 and April 1989; they lasted from 20 minutes to two hours, roughly 50 minutes on average.[44]

Characteristics of Respondents

The age breakdown of respondents was fairly even (table 1.A1), averaging between 21 and 22. More men than women were interviewed; women accounted for 41 percent of the sample.

According to information provided by the respondents, nearly 60 percent of them belonged to the upper and upper-middle classes, i.e., their parents were professionals, teachers and business people. More male students (66 percent) than female students (48 percent) had parents who belonged to this category of people.

Based on various indices (permanent address stated for university records, for example) 35 of the 75 respondents (47 percent) came from the immediate Quebec City region, and 29 (38 percent) from elsewhere.[45] It is worth noting that 91 percent of the respondents identified as coming from the Quebec City region lived with their parents; most of the remainder were tenants.[46]

Some 40 percent of respondents said they were working part time while attending school, slightly over 15 hours a week on average, although some worked up to 25 hours. There was no significant difference between the sexes on hours worked. A 1988 study at Université Laval revealed that 45.2 percent of the students were working part time. Over 30 percent of this group worked more than 30 hours a week (Bouchard 1990, 2).

The 1990 Inquiry

The second survey covered more students (1 008), since it was conducted by means of a multiple-choice questionnaire rather than individual interviews.[47] Again it should be stressed that this inquiry was carried out among high school students, unlike the first, which centred on university students. Furthermore, it is worth noting that 18 percent of the respondents were enrolled in a

Table 1.A1
Breakdown of respondents (1988 inquiry), by age

Age	N	%*
19	7	9.3
20	18	24.0
21	12	16.0
22	13	17.3
23	13	17.3
24	12	16.0
Total	75	99.9

Notes: Total sample = 75 Université Laval students.

*Percentage does not total 100.0 because of rounding.

Drummondville region school. Given the scope of the inquiry, it was carried out within a short time; the questionnaires were distributed in the eight schools between 17 May and 8 June 1990. These constraints prevented us from establishing a representative sample in the statistical sense of the word, although the range of young people in the selected schools displayed the diversity essential to this type of study (table 1.A2).

Before the questionnaire was distributed, students were informed of the objective of the research and given instructions on how to complete the questionnaire. The same information was given to all of the groups. One hour was allotted for completion of the questionnaire, though respondents were free to leave as soon as they had finished.[48]

Characteristics of Respondents

The students selected were enrolled in Secondary 4, or grade 11 (41 percent), and Secondary 5, grade 12 (59 percent).[49] As table 1.A3 indicates, they ranged from 15 to 20 years old, although most (96 percent) fell into the 16–18 age bracket. All told, 51 percent of the respondents were young women.

At the time of the study, more than a quarter (29 percent) of the students surveyed were enrolled in private schools, though only 27 percent had completed all or part of their studies there. This indicator, rather than the simple fact of being enrolled in a private school program at the time of the study, will be highlighted when differences are established between the two.

Table 1.A4 indicates the breakdown of the occupations of the respondents' fathers. They consisted primarily of upper- and middle-level managers and workers. This same hierarchy of occupations did not obtain among the mothers, a large proportion of whom were homemakers (38.6 percent). Mothers working outside the home were mainly employees or engaged in the intermediate professions (over 10 percent of the total).[50]

Table 1.A2
Secondary schools selected for the sample (1990 inquiry)

	%
École secondaire Les Etchemins	
Charny (south shore of Quebec City)	
Public	
Offers Secondary 3–5 (grades 10–12)	
2 020 students	
Urban and rural population	
Breakdown of sample from whole of Secondary 4	8.9
Breakdown of sample from whole of Secondary 5	17.1
Polyvalente La Camaradière	
Duberger/Les Saules (western part of Quebec City)	
Public	
1 300 students	
Blue-collar population	
Breakdown of sample from whole of Secondary 4	16.5
Breakdown of sample from whole of Secondary 5	9.1
Polyvalente de l'Ancienne-Lorette	
Ancienne-Lorette (near the northwestern suburbs of Quebec City)	
Public	
1 925 students	
Middle-income population	
Breakdown of sample from whole of Secondary 4	21.6
Breakdown of sample from whole of Secondary 5	13.7
École secondaire Les Compagnons de Cartier	
Sainte-Foy (near the western suburbs of Quebec City)	
Public	
1 865 students	
Middle- and upper-income population	
Breakdown of sample from whole of Secondary 4	21.1
Breakdown of sample from whole of Secondary 5	29.7
Collège Notre-Dame de Bellevue	
Quebec City	
Private (female students)	
800 students	
Middle- and upper-income population	
Breakdown of sample from whole of Secondary 4	34.5
Breakdown of sample from whole of Secondary 5	39.0
Juvénat Notre-Dame du Saint-Laurent	
Saint-Romuald (south shore of Quebec City)	
Private (male students)	
265 students	
Urban and rural population	
Breakdown of sample from whole of Secondary 4	73.0
Breakdown of sample from whole of Secondary 5	92.9

Table 1.A2 (cont'd)
Secondary schools selected for the sample (1990 inquiry)

	%
Collège de Lévis	
Lévis (south shore of Quebec City)	
Private (co-educational)	
850 students	
Urban and rural population	
Breakdown of sample from whole of Secondary 4	43.4
Breakdown of sample from whole of Secondary 5	38.4
Polyvalente Marie-Rivier	
Drummondville	
Public	
1 400 students	
Urban and rural population	
Breakdown of sample from whole of Secondary 4	4.0
Breakdown of sample from whole of Secondary 5	26.2
Total students surveyed	*(1 008)*

Table 1.A3
Breakdown of students (1990 inquiry), by age

Age	N	%
20	5	0.5
19	30	3.0
18	190	18.8
17	503	49.9
16	272	27.0
15	1	0.1
No response	7	0.7
Total	1 008	100.0

Note: Total sample = 1 008 secondary school students.

    Almost all of the young people in the sample said they were Roman Catholic (96.6 percent). However, differences were noted in religious practice: less than half of the respondents claimed to practise their religion "rarely" (44.3 percent); one-third said they "very regularly" or "fairly regularly" practised it. Equal numbers of female and male students claimed to practise their religion rarely, although more of the former than the latter very regularly or regularly did so.[51] No significant differences were noted on the basis of age.

Table 1.A4
Breakdown of respondents (1990 inquiry), by father's occupation

	N	%
Farmers	26	2.6
Artisans, commercial	100	10.2
Upper-level managers	271	27.6
Teachers, professors	57	5.8
Middle-level managers	190	19.3
Employees	155	15.8
Blue-collar workers	184	18.7
Total	983	100.0

Note: Total sample = 1 008 secondary school students.

Table 1.A5
Breakdown of respondents (1990 inquiry), according to part-time employment

	N	%
Does not work	416	41.3
Works less than 15 hours a week	367	36.4
Works more than 15 hours a week	222	22.0
No response	3	0.3
Total	1 008	100.0

Note: Total sample = 1 008 secondary school students.

Nearly 60 percent of the students surveyed said they were working part time in addition to attending school (table 1.A5), a significantly higher figure than that recorded for university students. This percentage is striking, especially as, for the same age group, it is also higher than in other inquiries. A 1984 survey conducted among 400 Secondary 4 (grade 11) students, representative of the Montreal region and a provincial town, revealed that nearly one-third (29.8 percent) of the respondents said they were working (Bouchard and Tremblay 1985, 59). According to the 1989 Segma-Lavalin survey, 40 percent of young people of the same age said they were working part time (*L'Actualité* 1989, 30).

The disparity in the findings of the various surveys raises a number of questions. Has the situation changed so much in just a few years, indeed, a few months? Did the wording of the questions introduce a bias? Did young people understand the term "part-time employment" in different ways, with some, for example, including babysitting, thereby referring more to "earning money" than holding a job? Be that as it may, in this study the type of job was a marginal factor. What is important is that, in addition to their studies, a high proportion of young people were engaged in remunerative activities.[52]

Part-time employment is an important reality of the everyday experience of many Quebec high school students. Over one-third of the respondents in our survey said they worked over 15 hours a week. More male students (66.3 percent) than female students (51.4 percent) claimed to have a job.

NOTES

This study was completed in September 1990.

The study is the result of two inquiries. The first, which took the form of interviews conducted among students at Université Laval, was funded by the Social Sciences and Humanities Research Council of Canada, whose support is gratefully acknowledged. The second and more extensive survey in eight high schools, involving 1 008 students, required the collaboration of many people in order to complete it in such a short time. We would particularly like to thank the secondary school principals who permitted the survey and the teachers who gave us an hour of classroom time at a very busy time of year. We would also like to thank Annick Percheron, director of the Centre d'étude de la vie politique française contemporaine (Fondation nationale des sciences politiques, Paris), who supervised the preparation of the questionnaire administered to high school students and who gave us permission to use a number of questions designed for her surveys. Solange Gariépy provided vital assistance in interviewing university students, and André Martel and Pierre Skilling handled the entry of data collected from high school students. Our thanks, as well, to all of the students who anonymously completed the questionnaire and shared their comments with us. Some of the respondents stated that the survey gave them an opportunity to reflect on these questions, which can only be a source of satisfaction to researchers.

In this study, quoted material that originated in French has been translated into English.

1. This *majority* figure is used throughout when claiming: "young people think ..."

2. The inquiries thus focus more precisely on a young student population. At the risk of repeating ourselves, the notion of youth encompasses several facets and we do not claim to examine all of them. However, it should be noted that, according to the latest Canada Census figures, nearly 80 percent of young people 17 years of age were enrolled full time in an educational institution; among 18-year-olds, this figure scarcely exceeds 50 percent (Canada, Statistics Canada 1989, 23). The most recent federal census revealed

that 25 percent of young Canadians in the 15–24 age bracket live in Quebec, compared with 36 percent in Ontario. There are roughly 243 000 males and 232 000 females in the 15–19 age bracket in Quebec.

3. In 1982, the average monthly unemployment rate among 15- to 24-year-olds in Quebec reached an all-time high of 23.4 percent; it has hovered around 17 percent for the past five years (Fortin 1986).

4. Gauthier (1990) has examined this question.

5. Benoît and Chauveau (1986) took a humorous look at this situation. The authors, who are young themselves, responded to their detractors with an unequivocal attack on the behaviour of their elders.

6. The sample for this inquiry was made up of 75 young students at Université Laval – the first third consisted of students in Political Science, the second third from the social sciences, and the remainder from other faculties. For details about the research methodology, see the Appendix.

7. The inquiry undertaken with Université Laval students was, as noted earlier, an opinion study; the figures provided in the tables should be considered as measurements of degree, and not as statistical measures in the strict sense of the term.

8. It should be made clear at this point that we are dealing only with a view of politics. We shall discuss participation in the second part of this study.

9. These are principles, it should be recalled, that are held not only by youth. A Gallup survey of July 1989 confirmed yet again that, for 46 percent of Canadians surveyed, the most important qualities for a prime minister are honesty and loyalty. The survey was conducted among 1 034 individuals representative of the Canadian population (*La Presse* 1989, A6).

10. For this inquiry, 1 008 students were surveyed, from the Quebec City and Drummondville regions, at the end of May and the beginning of June 1990. A little less than three-quarters of these students attended public schools. The survey methodology is detailed in the Appendix.

11. Only one-third of the young people felt interested; but this result is probably explained even by the wording of the question. In determining an interest in politics for the survey, the young people had to choose among the following four responses: "I am interested in politics and I participate actively in it"; "I am interested in politics but I do not participate actively in it"; "Politics does not interest me very much"; "Politics does not interest me at all." We have consolidated the first two responses (5 percent and 28 percent, respectively) to determine an interest in politics. The remaining 35 percent and 32 percent fall into the last two categories of the Foundation survey. For the 20- to 24-year-old age group, it should be noted, the proportion of interested young people is assumed to rise to 44 percent for the whole of Canada.

12. It should be noted that a greater proportion of blue-collar workers were the fathers of students who had attended mainly public schools (21.7 percent as compared to 10.4 percent). Conversely, more students who had attended mainly private schools reported their fathers as being in the senior management category (36.8 percent as compared to 24.1 percent).

13. A multiple regression indicates that for the children of managers on the one hand, and for those of blue-collar workers on the other, there is no significant relationship between sex and the fact of having studied in public or private school.

    For the sons and daughters of managers, we find:

    1. for sex, value of $F = 2.20$, significant at .1396;
    2. for educational sector, value of $F = 0.47$, significant at .4956.

    For the children of blue-collar workers, we find:

    1. for educational sector, value of $F = 2.67$, significant at .1041;
    2. for sex, value of $F = 2.22$, significant at .1041.

    Instead, the same type of analysis shows that for young men, but more particularly for young women, there is a significant relationship between the type of education and the father's work (blue-collar or managerial).

    For male students:

    1. for educational sector, value of $F = 0.1$, significant at .7467;
    2. for father's occupation (worker or manager), value of $F = 3.86$, significant at .0507.

    For female students:

    1. for father's occupation, value of $F = 3.15$, significant at .0772;
    2. for educational sector, value of $F = 6.95$, significant at .009.

14. We have rejected the term depoliticization, which implies a diminution of interest; this will be explained later.

15. In December 1985, 36 percent of 15- to 24-year-olds claimed to be interested in politics, compared with 41 percent of the population as a whole (Percheron 1987, 121).

16. Among numerous reference works in this domain, Mendel (1983) proposes an interesting approach.

17. See Fournier (1986). It is enough just to read or re-read certain writings to be convinced of this: "if the first technical revolution gave birth to the proletariat which made it disappear, the second confirmed the existence of youth whose specific task is to introduce into the world the virtue of a certain regenerative chaos" (Marier 1970, quoted in Jousselin 1977, 17).

18. Société Radio-Canada sponsored this 1964 study by Rioux and Sévigny. It dealt with the opinions and attitudes of young French-speaking resi-

dents of Quebec between the ages of 18 and 21. Over 800 people were surveyed. The findings were published in Rioux and Sévigny (1965).

19. The nature of the question requires the introduction of certain caveats. As Dumas et al. (1982) have noted, this type of indicator, encompassing such varied elements as work, friends or the family, tends de facto to relegate political participation to the bottom of the heap. "Endeavouring in this way to ascertain the expectations of college students," note the authors, "is to back up Saint-Exupéry's sarcasm about grownups who love figures, always without realizing that they hide more than they reveal" (ibid., 30). The authors do, however, cite a number of other studies which, while they show that "politics is not necessarily excluded from the predominant concerns of young people," nonetheless indicate that politics is of concern to a limited percentage of these young people.

20. Curiously enough, the same phenomenon was noted a few weeks prior to the events of November–December 1986 in France (see Hudon and Lecomte 1987).

21. "Good citizenship is not confined to a few lessons in understanding the function and importance of institutions, but it is the result of a process of integration into society; among the 18- to 20-year-olds, 20 percent of those who held a steady job abstained [from elections], while 33 percent of unemployed young people of the same age neglected their duties as citizens in 1986" (Carraud 1989, 142).

22. The wave of protest by university and high school students in 1986, which was as sudden as it was unexpected, opposed the university reforms proposed by the Jacques Chirac government which was in a strong position because of the Right's victory in the March 1986 legislative elections. The proposal, based on a neo-liberal philosophy, stipulated among other things that a selection would take place before students entered university, that university degrees would be created parallel to national degrees and that tuition fees would be increased. The proposal was withdrawn under pressure from the students and after the police killed a demonstrator. Alain Devaquet, minister of higher education, resigned. This social movement undermined the authority of the head of the government and put a halt to a series of new public policies which had scarcely been set in motion by the new government. On this question, see Hudon and Lecomte (1987).

23. The most cynical appeared to be Montrealers and young women.

24. The same shift is apparent in comparing the findings based on level of confidence toward political parties. Thus, 53 percent of the young people who do not have confidence in political parties feel rarely or never concerned about political decisions, while 66.7 percent of them state they are not interested in politics.

25. Among the young people who feel an affinity for a party and who would vote for the Parti québécois, one-half would choose the Progressive Conservative Party of Canada at the federal level, 20 percent the Liberal

Party of Canada, 15 percent the New Democratic Party and 14 percent refused to respond. For those who would vote for the Liberal Party of Quebec, two-thirds would choose the Liberal Party of Canada, 32 percent the Progressive Conservative Party of Canada, and 5 percent refused to respond (none would vote for the New Democratic Party).

26. Respondents were not asked which party they would vote for, since the majority of them were not yet of legal voting age.

27. This, too, is a noteworthy piece of information. Of course, in order to interpret it seriously we would have to analyse the general trend over several years, as the importance of the particular period in explaining voting patterns is well known. Nevertheless, this finding goes against traditional electoral sociology principles according to which new cohorts feel more attracted to opposition parties (which is certainly the case at the provincial level, but not at the federal level). This can perhaps be explained by the current political situation and discussion surrounding the national question (the survey was conducted in June 1990, several days before the failure of the Meech Lake accord). Can we see evidence here of a degree of political reflection among young people who, in favouring the Progressive Conservatives, would be making a certain choice?

28. Moreover, a majority of those whom the preceding indicators permit us to consider as interested in politics (according to the general index of non-interest in politics) also would not hesitate to undertake this type of activity.

29. It should be noted that no clarification was given in the questionnaire with respect to the type of election. These responses must not be interpreted in terms of political elections.

30. The question was: "To defend an idea in which you believe, would you be ready to ...?" (yes, certainly; yes, perhaps; no, not really; certainly not).

31. We have employed the terminology used in this survey.

32. Strictly speaking, however, it is difficult to make comparisons, since these figures are for all of Canada.

33. More than half of the young people work part time in addition to going to school (see Appendix for details).

34. For example, 5 percent of the young people in the 15 to 19 age bracket in the Canadian Youth Foundation survey claimed to be interested in politics and to participate actively in it. Active participation may encompass a broader range of activities than simply joining a political movement.

35. See the series of articles by Laurier (1985) commemorating the fiftieth anniversary of the Jeunesse étudiante catholique movement.

36. On the question of political socialization, see, among others, Percheron (1974) and Renshon (1977).

37. This expressed opinion comes far ahead of commitment to political parties

(12.5 percent fully agree that committing oneself to a party is the best way of ensuring that politics reflects their ideas), commitment to groups (15.5 percent), or the simple fact of expressing one's opinions publicly (38.9 percent).

38. A number of sociologists maintain that the right to vote is one of the last rites of passage into adulthood in industrialized societies.

39. The impact would probably be more psychological than real, moreover, since abstention from voting, it will be recalled, is in any case a significant phenomenon among young people. On these questions, see Coutrot (1967).

40. We are thinking in particular of the new international school in Sainte-Foy (Commission scolaire des Découvreurs), in suburban Quebec City, where time must be reserved for students to engage in community work with elderly people, groups experiencing problems, immigrants and so on.

41. During a recent symposium at Nancy, one of the officers of the Fédération française des Maisons de jeunes et de la culture (MJC) insisted on the essential role of sport as a "contribution to the model of a peaceful society" and wondered if young people's great infatuation with this type of participatory activity was not linked, in part, to the possibility of really living this model.

42. Benoît-Paul Hébert was largely responsible for carrying out this inquiry. At the outset, we decided to set up three distinct groups of 100 respondents, depending on the field of study, as we postulated that this indicator would affect perceptions of politics: one group was made up of students enrolled in a political science program; the second was made up of students enrolled in a social sciences program other than political science, e.g., anthropology, economics, psychology, industrial relations, social services and sociology; the third was made up of students enrolled in programs other than the social sciences. The three groups, each made up of 100 students, were set up randomly from a computerized list of students enrolled at Université Laval. The students selected had to be under 25 years of age, be studying full time in an undergraduate program lasting two years or more, i.e., be registered for at least 12 credits in a program comprising at least 60 credits (specialized bachelor's program, bachelor's degree with major and minor or diploma), and be a Canadian citizen.

We then divided each of the three lists of 100 names into 25 subgroups, each containing four names, within which the last three persons served as substitutes, in the event the person contacted was unavailable for the interview. The response rate was 59 percent for the three lists overall (it does not take into account the persons we were unable to reach because they were absent for a prolonged period or had moved, because we failed to obtain a response after the fourth call, or the person failed to return our call). Striking variations in the rate appeared depending on the field of study: it was 76 percent among students enrolled in political science, 59 percent among those in the social sciences and 49 percent for the other faculties. Does this suggest there is a close link between the fact that a student is enrolled in political science and therefore has an apparently greater interest in politics or, at least, a greater opportunity to talk about politics? We must not overlook the fact that the head of the research project, who was director of the department at the time, was known to political science students.

43. As Donegani et al. have pointed out (1980, 15), "[respondents in this type of survey] cannot be chosen according to representativity criteria in the statistical sense. On the contrary, it is in the interest of researchers to select respondents on the basis of the greatest possible diversity of assumed attitudes about the theme of the study, according to variables which are thought to play a role in structuring the field to be explored."

44. Respondents were interviewed by the same two people, who wrote down their comments. All of the material assembled was analysed by one of them and verified by the other.

45. Eleven doubtful cases were not classified according to place of origin.

46. The place of origin of the respondents is not a neutral-given when it is compared with other data on the status of the respondents. Among the students who appeared to come from the Quebec City region, males outnumbered females two to one; among the other students, the sexes are more or less equal. Moreover, while a majority of the students (57 percent) from the Quebec City region said they had a job, only a minority (21 percent) of the remainder made such a statement.

47. This is called a closed questionnaire. For further information, see the collective work directed by Selltiz (1977), or Grawitz (1976). Bernard Fournier and Raymond Hudon were responsible for the inquiry, and Louis Métivier administered the questionnaire and looked after a large part of the compilation of the data.

48. Most of the students answered the 87 questions in 40 minutes.

49. Most of the students were in history and geography classes. Because of time and scheduling constraints, in some schools students in French, economics or religious and moral education classes were also surveyed.

50. Mainly nurses or management secretaries.

51. More precisely, 35.9 percent of female students compared with 28.5 percent of male students.

52. The disparities depend on the age of the respondents. The majority of 16-year-old students are not working part time (54.8 percent), but this percentage decreases the older the students are (38.6 percent for 17-year-olds, and 31.1 percent among 18-year-olds). Some 52 percent of young people in Secondary 4 (grade 11) appear to be employed, compared with 64 percent in Secondary 5 (grade 12).

REFERENCES

L'Action nationale. 1990. "Si la jeunesse était une richesse." 80 (April).

L'Actualité. 1989. "Les valeurs des jeunes." (June): 28–48.

AÉÉSPUL (Association des étudiants et des étudiantes en science politique de l'Université Laval). 1986. *La place des jeunes dans la société politique québécoise.* Montreal: Association canadienne-française pour l'avancement des sciences.

Bélanger, Louis. 1986. "Pratiques politiques des jeunes dans une société en mutation." In *La place des jeunes dans la société politique québécoise,* ed. AÉÉSPUL. Montreal: Association canadienne-française pour l'avancement des sciences.

Benoît, François, and Philippe Chauveau. 1986. *Acceptation globale; ta Volvo contre mon B.S.* Montreal: Boréal.

Bibby, Reginald W., and Donald C. Posterski. 1985. *The Emerging Generation: An Inside Look at Canada's Teenagers.* Toronto: Irwin.

Blouin, Jean. 1984. "Les valeurs des jeunes." *L'Actualité* (May): 39–46.

Bouchard, Alain. 1990. "De 30 à 40 heures de boulot s'ajoutent au temps d'étude." *Le Soleil,* 17 September.

Bouchard, Pierre, and Henri Tremblay. 1985. *Avoir 15 ou 16 ans en 1985. Inventaire des activités socio-culturelles des jeunes.* Quebec: Ministère de l'Éducation.

Bourdieu, Pierre. 1980. *Questions de sociologie.* Paris: Éditions de Minuit.

Camilleri, Carmel, and Claude Tapia. 1983. *Les nouveaux "jeunes"; la politique ou le bonheur.* Toulouse: Privat.

Canada. Statistics Canada. 1989. *Youth in Canada: Selected Highlights.* Cat. 89-511. Ottawa: Minister of Supply and Services Canada.

Canadian Youth Foundation. 1989. *Canada's Youth: "Ready for Today."* Ottawa: Minister of State for Youth.

Carraud, Michel. 1989. *Que faire des jeunes? ... radiographie d'une nouvelle fracture sociale ...* Paris: Publisud.

Coutrot, Aline. 1967. "Les jeunes entrent en politique." *Projet* 115:521–31.

Donegani, Jean-Marie, Guy Michelat and Michel Simon. 1980. *Représentations du champ social, attitudes politiques et changements socio-économiques.* Paris/Lille: CÉVIPOF/Institut de sociologie.

Dumas, Suzanne, Gérard Rochais and Henri Tremblay. 1982. *Une génération silencieusement lucide? Vers un profil socio-culturel des jeunes de 15 à 20 ans.* Quebec: Ministère de l'Éducation.

Dumont, Fernand, ed. 1986. *Une société des jeunes?* Quebec: Institut québécois de recherche sur la culture.

Fortin, Pierre. 1986. "Conjoncture, démographie et politique: où va le chômage des jeunes au Québec?" In *Une société des jeunes?* ed. Fernand Dumont. Quebec: Institut québécois de recherche sur la culture.

Fournier, Bernard. 1986. "Jeunesse et changement social: un mythe?" In *La place des jeunes dans la société politique québécoise,* ed. AÉÉSPUL. Montreal: Association canadienne-française pour l'avancement des sciences.

———. 1989. *Mouvements de jeunes et socialisation politique: la dynamique de la J.É.C. à l'époque de Gérard Pelletier.* Quebec: Université Laval, Laboratoire d'études politiques et administratives.

Fournier, Bernard, and Franck Pépratx. 1991. "La majorité politique: étude des débats sur la fixation d'un seuil." In *Âge et politique,* ed. Annick Percheron and René Rémond. Paris: Économica.

Gauthier, Madeleine. 1990. "Diversité des rythmes d'entrée des jeunes sur le marché du travail." *L'Action nationale* 80 (April): 482–93.

Grawitz, Madeleine. 1976. *Méthodes des sciences sociales.* Paris: Dalloz.

Hudon, Raymond, and Patrick Lecomte. 1987. *L'engagement sans médiations: auto-analyse du mouvement étudiant de l'automne 1986 en France.* Quebec: Université Laval, Laboratoire d'études politiques et administratives.

Joffrin, Laurent. 1987. *Un coup de jeune: portrait d'une génération morale.* Paris: Arléa.

Jousselin, Jean. 1977. *Enfants perdus ou éclaireurs?* Paris: Flammarion.

Laurier, Marie. 1985. "Une véritable école de chefs." *Le Devoir,* 17 October.

Marier, Gérard. 1970. *L'avenir des étudiants et les étudiants de l'avenir.* Trois-Rivières: Les Presses de l'Université du Québec à Trois-Rivières.

Mendel, Gérard. 1983. *54 millions d'individus sans appartenance; l'obstacle invisible du septennat: essai de psychopolitique.* Paris: Robert Laffont.

Pelletier, Gérard. 1948. "Scrupules ou inertie?" *Le Devoir,* 31 January.

———. 1985. "La J.É.C. des années 30: Un vin nouveau." *La Presse,* 19 October.

Percheron, Annick. 1974. *L'univers politique des enfants.* Paris: Armand Collin et Fondation nationale des sciences politiques.

———. 1987. "Les jeunes et la politique ou la recherche d'un nouveau civisme." In *Jeunes d'aujourd'hui: regards sur les 13–25 ans en France.* Paris: La Documentation française.

Percheron, Annick, and René Rémond, eds. 1991. *Âge et politique.* Paris: Économica.

Petrowski, Nathalie. 1985. "Le militantisme: des grandes luttes collectives aux combats plus ponctuels et plus modestes." *Le Devoir*, 31 January.

La Presse. 1989. "Honnêteté et loyauté avant tout." 31 August.

Renshon, Stanley Allen, ed. 1977. *Handbook of Political Socialization*. New York: Free Press.

Rezsohazy, Rudolf. 1983. *Les jeunes: un profil social, politique et religieux*. Louvain-la-Neuve: Université catholique de Louvain.

Rioux, Marcel, and Robert Sévigny. 1965. *Les nouveaux citoyens: enquête sociologique sur les jeunes du Québec*. Montreal: Service des publications de Radio-Canada.

Schwartz, Bertrand. 1981. *Insertion professionnelle et sociale des jeunes, rapport au Premier ministre*. Paris: La Documentation française.

Selltiz, Claire. 1977. *Les méthodes de recherche en sciences sociales*. Montreal: Éditions HRW.

Touraine, Alain. 1986. "D'un coup de pied, le plongeur ..." *Le Monde*, 30 December.

Unesco. 1981. *La jeunesse dans les années 80*. Paris: Presses de l'Unesco.

Zarka, Pierre. 1983. *Jeunesse en quête d'avenir*. Paris: Messidor-Éditions sociales.

2

REVISITING THE VOTING AGE ISSUE UNDER THE CANADIAN CHARTER OF RIGHTS AND FREEDOMS

~

Patrice Garant

WITH A SINGLE stroke, legislators may lower the voting age to 17 or 16. But why would they do so? To meet a requirement of the *Canadian Charter of Rights and Freedoms?* To involve young people more closely in the political process? To accommodate a trend in legislation that gives individuals under 18 years of age responsibilities, and assigns them rights and obligations?

To date there has been little interest in this question. In his work on electoral law, Boyer (1981, 125) devotes one line to it. In his collected writings on the Charter, Beaudoin (1989) devotes half a page to the question. He believes that the Charter is deficient in not setting a voting age. On the other hand, he thinks that the age of 18, which corresponds to the age of majority set by the provincial legislatures, "appears reasonable." As to concern about the disparity in British Columbia where the age of majority is 19, he observes that it "appears marginal" (1989, 272). Few other authors have broached the issue.[1]

No research appears to have been done on the issue of the voting age at Elections Canada or at the Office of the Chief Electoral Officer of Quebec. The latter's *Statutory Report* (Quebec, Chief Electoral Officer 1983, 97) devotes a few lines to it.

The British Columbia Royal Commission on Electoral Reform was given a mandate in 1976 to consider the issue. In its final report (1978), it described the results of an opinion poll held during its public hearings. Fifty-five percent of participants were in favour of lowering the voting age from 19 to 18. The main argument appeared to be that the voting age in British Columbia should match the voting age for federal elections and the age of majority in the other provinces. The Commission rejected this argument as specious. It suspected that the federal situation was rather the result of "pure political play." The Commission argued that "it is obvious that there is no one age which can be identified as the time when young people mature sufficiently to enable them to cast intelligent votes or to be politically concerned, for that matter" (British Columbia, Royal Commission 1978, 187). The Commission was, moreover, not convinced that the age of 18 was in any way an improvement over 19, because during the hearings no significant majority was in favour of the change.

Several pages are dedicated to the issue in federal and provincial parliamentary debates, but these do not give the impression that detailed studies were carried out on the subject, as we shall see later in this study.

In the United States, the question of the voting age generated heated debate during the 1970s. It was inevitable that the issue should surface some day because the American Constitution defers to state legislation on the right to vote in both state and federal elections. Differences between various statutes have in the past given rise to legal disputes, including the famous Supreme Court decision *Oregon v. Mitchell* (1970);[2] Congress responded by enacting the Twenty-sixth Amendment in 1971. Doctrine is nevertheless scarce for these years, and the major American works on constitutional law have devoted only a few lines to the issue of the voting age (Stone et al. 1986, 756–57; Nowak et al. 1986, 722; Tribe 1988, 1055).

Before the proclamation of the *Canadian Charter of Rights and Freedoms* in 1982, legislators had complete discretion to set the voting age. But since the advent of the Charter, this definition of powers must be seen to conform with section 3 of that document, which states that "every citizen of Canada has the right to vote." Further, section 15 prohibits discrimination on the basis of age.

The Charter does, however, permit legislators to curtail constitutional rights, provided that such curtailment is reasonable and justified within the framework of a free and democratic society (section 7).

Legislators must make a choice that is political in nature, even though it may be contested in the courts. This choice may be made by considering all the related law and the way in which the age of majority or minority is used to satisfy various social, economic and cultural ends.

It is of prime consideration, however, that encouragement to participate in the democratic process should be given to all citizens who have a sufficient level of maturity to make enlightened decisions. The question that must be answered is whether this level is reached at age 18, or whether it is reached earlier.

If we look at the body of electoral law, as well as the numerous statutes of a social or economic nature, we can gain a good understanding about legislators' attitudes toward young people aged 16 or 17 – a group to whom they do not hesitate to assign important responsibilities. If young people are thus accorded such trust in various fields of activity, why should they be prevented from participating more fully in the democratic process? Consider, in this respect, the attitude of political parties, whose policies permit a relatively high level of participation by young people.

The response of the courts to this question would not be unequivocal. Judges must take into account the impact that lowering the voting age below 18 would have on electoral law, on civil and criminal law, as well as on a host of laws of an economic and social nature. In addition, judges must operate within the framework of the Charter.

ELECTORAL STATUTES

General Electoral Statutes

With the exception of British Columbia's provincial legislation, all federal and provincial electoral statutes set the voting age at 18 for provincial and federal elections. This corresponds with the age of majority established by provincial legislatures on matters under their jurisdiction with respect to "Property and Civil Rights in the Province" (*Constitution Act, 1867* s. 92¶13). The correspondence between the civil age of majority and the voting age is striking (Canada, House of Commons 1969–70; 1970, 1543).

Two questions may be raised at this point. First, how did the legislatures justify such concordance? Second, are the reasons for setting a particular age of majority the same as those for setting a specific voting age?

It was during the 1969–70 parliamentary session that the *Canada Elections Act* was amended to lower the voting age from 21 to 18. Private members' bills had advocated such a change for about a dozen years, but in 1963 the Standing Committee on Privileges and Elections had unanimously approved such a measure.

In the 1969–70 session, the Committee and the House unanimously applauded such a reform, which was designed to encourage the participation of young people in the democratic process, lower the overall age of the electorate, and so on (Canada, House of Commons 1969–70; 1970, 1543). However, nowhere in the dozens of pages of deliberations on the issue can a rational and cogent argument be found to support the proposed reform. What in 1969 made young people who were 18 years of age capable of voting when they had not been earlier? Several members cited precedents from a number of provinces, including Quebec, Saskatchewan and Manitoba. It is interesting to note that at the end of 1969, the voting age was still 21 in three provinces (New Brunswick, Ontario and Nova Scotia) and 19 in three others (British Columbia, Alberta and Newfoundland) (Qualter 1970, 20).

In our opinion, lowering the federal voting age to 18 was the result of what on the surface was a clear trend, or fashion. One member of Parliament also noted the example of Britain, which had implemented the same reform following a 1967 report. The *Canada Elections Act* made an important exception, however, with respect to the voting age. Section 21 of Schedule II of the Act allows service personnel who are not 18 years of age to vote. Section 20 of the *National Defence Act* provides for the enlistment of young persons less than 18 years of age with parental consent.

In Quebec, MNAs have had at least three occasions to discuss the voting age since it was lowered to 18. In 1978, during discussion of the *Referendum Act*, reference was simply made to the *Election Act* (Quebec, Assemblée nationale, *Débats* 1978, B-4926). In 1984, when a new election act was passed, members were content to accede once again to the status quo (Quebec, Assemblée nationale 1984, B-16).[3] Finally, in May 1988, when the current *Election Act* was passed, no comment was made about the voting age; it apparently never occurred to anyone to do so.

Municipal and School Board Election Statutes
Municipal legislation in every province except British Columbia sets the municipal voting age at 18. There is therefore a clear trend toward aligning the voting age for local elections with the *Canada Elections Act* and adopting the civil age of majority. Once every province has abolished municipal electoral qualifications such as the requirement to be a property owner or tenant, and the right to vote has been given to every resident in a municipality, all adult residents will have the right to vote.

For school board elections, statutes were based on municipal laws and also adopted the age of majority in granting the right to vote to all residents. To our knowledge, no one has ever considered giving the right to vote to anyone younger than 18.

CIVIL AND CRIMINAL STATUTES
Civil and criminal statutes were the first to attribute a special place to young people in society. They are indicative of the basic concept of maturity adopted by legislators.

Civil Statutes
The *Civil Code of Lower Canada* and corresponding statutes from other provinces set the age of majority at 18. The Code states that "The incapacity of minors ... is established in their favour" (art. 987). The incapacity in question refers to the fact that they are not capable of contracting. This rule about the incapacity to contract and to manage property does not, according to case law, mean a general incapacity, but rather provides protection against injury (Tancelin 1988). The proposed new *Civil Code* for Quebec is even clearer on this issue: articles 170 to 172 of Bill 20 determine the minor's capacity with respect to an injury as a function of his age and judgement.

The Quebec *Code of Civil Procedure* prescribes that the minor shall have the assistance of a guardian (art. 56); case law has determined that the absence of such assistance constitutes a relative nullity that is designed to protect the incapacitated person (*Rimouski* 1981).[4]

The issue of the marriage of minors is different, however, because although the *Civil Code of Lower Canada* confers the right to be married on a young man at the age of 14 and on a young woman at the age of 12, it requires the consent of the father or mother (art. 115, 119), or of the guardian. Since 1987, the *Civil Code of Quebec* has set the age at which marriage may be contracted at 18 (art. 402), but it authorizes the court to "grant a dispensation where an intended spouse is not less than 16 years of age" (art. 403). A marriage contracted without judicial dispensation may be annulled, but no later than after one year has elapsed from the time the age condition has been fulfilled (art. 429).

One of the conditions of adoption in the *Civil Code of Quebec* is that the person adopting must be of full age (art. 598). It is generally required that a person be of full age to consent to the adoption of his or her own child, but the Code makes an exception by specifying that a parent who is a minor may so consent without authorization (art. 606). It is also worth noting that a child of 14 may refuse adoption (art. 602).

An Act respecting the change of name requires the consent of any unemancipated minor of 14 years of age or more to an application by the parents for a name change. To effect a change of name or sex, however, a person must be of full age.

One of the major effects of being of full age is the end of parental authority (Quebec, *Civil Code of Quebec*, art. 646). Unemancipated minors remain under parental supervision and cannot leave the family home without consent (art. 650). The person having parental authority has a right to correct a child with moderation and within reason (art. 651). If difficulties arise, the person having parental authority may refer the matter to the court, which will decide in the interest of the child (art. 653). The court may deprive the parents of such authority on the motion of any interested person and transfer such authority elsewhere (art. 654). Taken together, these provisions create an absolute dependence of minors, even those of 17 or 16 years of age.

The *Civil Code of Lower Canada*, under the title "of the enjoyment of civil rights," deals with the disposal of parts of the human body and medical experimentation; to do so a minor must have the authorization of a judge of the Superior Court and the consent of the person having parental authority (art. 20). The same requirement applies to the making of funeral arrangements and the disposal of remains, for which only the consent of the parents is required (art. 21).

Minority status ends with the emancipation that results automatically by marriage or by the decision of a court on the advice of a family counsel (art. 314–15): in the latter instance, however, a guardian must be appointed. In addition, unemancipated minors are in some instances treated as persons of full age, notably when they are bankers or tradespeople; this is also the case in regard to their obligations for civil offences (art. 1001ff.).

It can be seen that the position of minors under the civil law is ambivalent. The civil law deems minors to be incapable persons, but does so to protect them against injury. It does not absolutely prohibit minors from contracting or going to court. Few actions are absolutely prohibited – for example, adoption. Even the marriage of a 16- to 18-year-old minor contracted without judicial dispensation remains valid if it is not challenged within the time provided.

The civil laws in other Canadian provinces contain standards that are relatively analogous to those in Quebec. Here are a few examples.

In Alberta, where the age of majority is set at 18, the *Marriage Act* sets the marriageable age at 16, but adds that between the ages of 16 and 18, the consent of the parental authority or the Superior Court is required. The *Insurance Act* provides that 16-year-old minors are deemed to be of full age with respect to life insurance policies except for their rights as beneficiaries (s. 364); at age 16, minors may insure their own life or consent that their life be insured independently. In Alberta, a person 16 years of age or more is authorized to be served process or documents (Alberta, *Provincial Courts Act*, s. 42; *Employment Pension Plans Act*, s. 63); likewise, a person who appears to be at least 16 years of age may be served an order to proceed to an inspection under section 12 of the *Fire Prevention Act*.

In British Columbia, where the age of majority is 19, the same provisions are contained in the *Insurance Act* for minors who are 16 years of age. Provisions on the serving of process, documents or inspection orders to persons 16 years of age or more are also included in various acts (British Columbia, *Small Claims Act*; *Weed Control Act*). A young person 16 years of age may also act as a witness in a land transfer under the *Land Title Act*.

Criminal Law and Related Statutes

The criminal law makes frequent reference to age. Section 13 of the *Criminal Code* of Canada sets 12 years as the age at which a person is criminally responsible for his or her actions. On the other hand, the *Young Offenders Act* deems that a person is an adolescent between the ages of 12 and 18 and is subject to a system of law enforcement and detention that differs from that for adults aged 18.

The category of young persons of special interest to us is entitled to particular protection under the *Young Offenders Act*. A young person is tried by a youth court, but may be referred to an ordinary court by a court order "in the interest of society and having regard to the needs of the young person" (s. 16). If the young person is found guilty, the court may make any dispositions provided for in section 20 of the Act, the maximum penalty being three years in open custody or secure custody in the event of a serious offence (s. 24.1). The federal statute therefore establishes for minors a special protection system whose objective is indisputably rehabilitation rather than punishment.

The *Criminal Code* grants special protection to minors for sexual offences. For example, section 159 criminalizes anal intercourse for persons under 18 years of age, even where there is consent. Also, in the suppression of procuring, prostitution and related offences, the sentence is much stiffer when the person in question is under 18 years of age (s. 212(2),(4)). Legislators thus provide increased protection against the sexual exploitation of young people.

The *Criminal Code* criminalizes the abuse of a position of trust or authority for sexual purposes with adolescents from 14 to 18 years of age (s. 148). It also contains provisions on bawdy houses and the corruption of children, to protect those under age 18 (ss. 171–72).

One of the rare instances in which the *Criminal Code* treats 16- to 18-year-olds the same as adults is in the offence provided for in section 215 – that is, the duty of a father, mother or guardian to provide the necessaries of life. In the Code as a whole, however, young people aged 16 to 18 are given consideration that is comparable to if not greater than that provided by the *Civil Code of Lower Canada*.

The *Criminal Code*, on the other hand, gives those who are 16 years old and over the full right to carry firearms, except for restricted weapons: consent of the person with parental authority is only required for those under 16 years of age for weapons intended for hunting or other sporting activities. Provincial statutes on hunting do not appear to include restrictions except for persons under age 16. For example, the Alberta *Wildlife Act* prohibits persons under 16 from hunting with a firearm unless accompanied by a person with parental authority.

SOCIAL, ECONOMIC AND EDUCATION STATUTES

Social Statutes

The *Youth Protection Act* of Quebec is the most important of the social statutes. For example, legislators intended this Act to assure the security or development of children when they are threatened (s. 2). The Act applies to every child under 18 years of age (s. 1). It therefore establishes for young people a special system that is designed to protect them against any mistreatment of which they are sometimes the victims from third parties and, more particularly, from a member of their family.

When the security or development of the child is threatened, the Director of Youth Protection (DYP) may, where it is deemed necessary, apply various provisional measures such as removing the child from his or her environment and entrusting the child to a reception centre, a foster family, a hospital centre, an appropriate body or any other person (Quebec, *Youth Protection Act*, s. 46). The DYP may in less serious cases apply voluntary measures, such as keeping the child in his or her milieu and requiring the parents to make periodic reports on what measures are in place to correct the situation, and ensuring that the child is referred to appropriate care, assistance or counselling (s. 54).

Where voluntary measures are involved, the DYP, in communication with parents and the child for the purpose of reaching an agreement with them on the most appropriate measures, must inform any child of 14 years of age or more, and the child's parents, of their right to refuse the application of a measure (Quebec, *Youth Protection Act*, s. 52). Legislators have therefore given the 14-year-old child the power to make decisions that resembles the power of the adult parent. Such ability to intervene forces the DYP to attempt to reach agreement on new measures or to refer the child's situation to the court (s. 52) in instances where the child's safety remains compromised (s. 53.1).

The youth protection legislation studied applies to young persons at risk and who need help or protection. The latitude allowed to minors varies from province to province in the measures that can be taken by the person responsible for the protection of young people. In British Columbia, the young person must in all instances comply with the decision of the person in charge of youth protection, whereas in Quebec and Ontario, the young person may oppose the decision with respect to voluntary measures. A young person from Quebec may oppose such measures from the age of 14, while one from Ontario may only do so at 16 (Ontario, *Child and Family Services Act*, s. 31).

In the other provinces, statutes on children in need of protection apply to minors – that is, to those who are less than 18 years of age (19 in British Columbia) (Ontario, *Child and Family Services Act*; British Columbia, *Family and Child Service Act*). In Nova Scotia, however, it applies to those less than 16 years of age (Nova Scotia, *Children's Services Act*, c. 68).

The federal *Family Allowances Act* sets the age at which children are no longer eligible for allowances at 18 (s. 3).

In Quebec, the *Act respecting family assistance allowances* generally sets 18 as the age from which a single person is entitled to assistance, unless the person is married or the parent of a dependent child. In Ontario, a young person 16 to 21 years of age is entitled to social assistance if not attending an educational institution for reasons of physical or mental incapacity; this also applies if the young person has one or more dependent children. In Nova Scotia, where the age of majority is 19, the *Family Maintenance Act* sets the age of eligibility for assistance at 19. Note that the Nova Scotia Court of Appeal has determined that this provision does not apply to children, even if they are 16 years of age and have a dependent child (*McInnis* 1990).

In Alberta, some social legislation ceases to provide protection at the age of 16. This is the case in the *Maintenance and Recovery Act*, which provides for possible payment of allowances to those under 16 years of age unless they are students or intellectually handicapped. The *Manpower Development Act* covers young persons 16 years of age and over with respect to apprenticeship contracts. The *Maintenance Order Act* establishes an obligation to provide support for children less than 16 years of age, which would indicate that a person is assumed to be responsible for his or her own livelihood after the age of 16. The *International Child*

Abduction Act, which was enacted under the United Nations Convention on the Civil Aspects of International Child Abduction, covers only children less than 16 years of age. The *Alberta Income Tax Act* (s. 10) is applicable to young persons who are 16 years of age and over. The *Women's Institute Act* allows women 16 years of age and over to get together and establish an "institute" to pursue the various social and philanthropic goals provided for in the Act.

In British Columbia, section 19 of the *Mental Health Act* states that a young person 16 years of age may request admittance to a mental health institution. The *Infants Act* (s. 16) has provisions to allow young persons who are 16 to consent to surgical, medical, mental or dental health care. Also, the *Municipal Act* (s. 513) prohibits any licensee from doing business, providing services, selling or destroying goods in a manner that would endanger the health or safety of a young person less than 16 years of age; legislators therefore assume that those 16 to 18 years of age do not require such protection. A pawnbroker may not hire a person of less than 16 years of age to engage in the trade (*Pawnbrokers Act*).

In Manitoba, a young person 16 years of age is treated as an adult for the purpose of providing a service or completing work under the *Child and Family Services Act* (s. 108). When determining what benefits are to be paid to dependants of deceased workers, only children of less than 16 years of age are included.

Legislation that is related to school or education is among the most important of the group of social statutes, and requires children to attend school until the age of 16 in most provinces (Ontario, Quebec, Alberta) or 15 (British Columbia). This is extremely interesting, because legislators consider that beyond this age, the young person enters the labour force or continues studies at institutions of higher learning.

Economic Statutes

There are no statutes setting a lower age limit for engaging in an economic activity, that is, an activity other than one that is purely social or cultural. There are, however, requirements for persons 18 years of age or less when the activities in which they engage involve risks or consequences.

The first of such laws, which is typical of a highly industrialized consumer society, is the *Highway Safety Code* of Quebec (formerly the *Highway Code*). Minors who are 16 years old may obtain a driver's permit for any type of vehicle and own and register a vehicle in their own name; parental consent is needed unless they are emancipated or engaged in business.[5] Drivers are fully responsible for damage caused by their vehicle, except in the case of personal injury, for which the government plan provides compensation. Drivers are also responsible for ensuring that passengers under 16 wear seat belts. In Alberta, a young person of 16 may obtain a driver's permit, take out an insurance policy and drive another insured vehicle. Drivers are also required to ensure that passengers under 16 wear their seat belts, and a person must be 16 in order to buy or sell a motorbike.

Federal and Quebec statutes on business corporations generally set 18 as the age at which one can be a member of a board of directors (Canada, *Canada Business Corporations Act*, s. 105; Quebec, *Companies Act*, s. 123.73). For associations and cooperatives, provincial legislation sets 16 as the age required to be a member, though in general, 18 is the legal age to be elected to a board (Alberta, *Co-operative Associations Act*, ss. 20–24; Manitoba, *Credit Unions and Caisses Populaires Act*, s. 56). In Quebec, a minor must be at least 16 years of age to be a founder, member or board member of a cooperative (Quebec, *Co-operatives Act*). In Quebec, college students, even if they are minors, may be elected to the board of governors of their institutions or assume other official functions (Quebec, *General and Vocational Colleges Act*).

Many statutes and regulations on the professions do not set any age limit for engaging in a profession or trade. Some, however, as in Quebec, require that a permit holder be 18 years of age to be a real estate broker (Quebec, *Regulation respecting the application of the Real Estate Brokerage Act*, r. 1) or a building contractor (Quebec, *An Act respecting building contractors vocational qualifications*, s. 32).

Provincial legislation on outlets for alcoholic beverages and for the purchase and consumption of alcohol uses the age of majority, normally 18, as the age at which this activity is permitted; in some provinces, including Nova Scotia and British Columbia, the age is 19.

In British Columbia, the *Wildlife Act* (s. 13) requires that any person 16 years of age and over must possess a permit to engage in sport fishing. The *Fisheries Act* (s. 8) places the same obligation on persons 16 years of age for fishing in general. The law also permits a person 16 years of age involved in "management, cost or industrial accounting or business organization and management" to become a member of the Accountants Association (British Columbia, *Accountants (Management) Act*, s. 4).

In Manitoba, income tax legislation considers any person 16 years of age and over whose principal residence is in Manitoba to be a provincial taxpayer (Manitoba, *Income Tax Act*, s. 4.1).

All economic statutes confer many rights on young people aged 16 to 18. In Quebec when such persons are in the labour market, all labour legislation applies to them, including the *Labour Code, An Act respecting industrial accidents* and the *Act respecting labour standards*. Since attendance at school up to age 16 is no longer mandatory (under certain conditions), many young people find themselves in the labour market.

It is symptomatic of our society that all economic statutes, particularly those concerning work and participation in economic activity, should apply to young persons 16 years of age or older; minors involved in business are included with those of full age, and young workers are treated on an equal footing with adults. Economic activity is extremely important today, as was recognized by the Supreme Court in its determinations pursuant to section 2(*b*) of the Charter, in which it placed freedom of expression in economic and business matters on an equal footing with political and religious freedom (*Ford* 1988; *Reference re ss. 193 and 195.1(1)(c) of the Criminal Code (Man.)* 1990).

Statutes Applying to Students

Some provincial and even some federal statutes concern students who attend post-secondary educational institutions (colleges and universities). However, there does not appear to be a minimum age for entrance into these institutions, or a minimum age for access to programs for students, such as financial assistance and scholarships. Some financial-aid statutes specifically include both students who are minors and students who are of full age (Nova Scotia, *Student Aid Act*).

In Quebec, the *Act respecting the accreditation and financing of student associations* is of particular interest with regard to the political rights of young people. This Act applies to both university- and college-level institutions. Quebec students can therefore assert their rights both within their institutions and vis-à-vis the government from the age of 16.

Official status is conferred on student associations (ibid, s. 8) through a democratic accreditation process (s. 6). The educational institution is from that time on required to recognize the accredited association as the representative of the institution's students. The association is also empowered to collect fees from students to finance its operations (s. 52).

The Act not only enshrines freedom of association for students, but also makes it possible for them to give themselves effective ways to assert their rights in their dealings with various levels of authority.

It is noteworthy that this Act gives political rights to young persons under 18 years of age, insofar as the average age is 16 at which students enter a Cegep (General and Vocational College). It is interesting to compare this with the political rights conferred on young people of this age in provincial and federal politics.

It is also interesting to note that political parties generally accept young people under 18 as regular members. The Progressive Conservative and Liberal parties of Canada allow young people of 14 to become members and to vote on the various issues. Their respective youth committees set the rules for involvement in the various bodies. At the provincial level, at least in Quebec, the two major parties, the Quebec Liberal party (QLP) and the Parti québécois (PQ), have set the age for party membership at 16. In the QLP, young persons less than 26 years of age are included in the youth committee, which makes the rules for voting on various issues; the PQ's organization appears to be identical.

CONSTITUTIONAL ASPECTS OF THE AGE ISSUE

Until 1982, legislators had full discretion to set the voting age. The advent of the *Canadian Charter of Rights and Freedoms* altered the situation. Section 3 of the Charter makes the right to vote and to be a candidate in federal and provincial elections a constitutionally entrenched right that cannot be affected even by the notwithstanding clauses: section 33, for example, does not apply to section 3. However, as the Supreme Court has determined, none of these entrenched rights is absolute; according to section 1, they may be subject to such reasonable limits prescribed by law as can be demonstrably justified in a free and democratic society. Moreover, section 15 of the Charter creates an equality right and prohibits any discrimination based on age and other factors.

A priori, restricting the right to vote to citizens 18 years of age or more is an infringement of section 3 of the Charter and therefore constitutes discrimination based on age. Whereas until 1982 legislators could set the voting age more or less arbitrarily, they now must justify their reasons. Governments, in compliance with the case law of the Supreme Court of Canada, must be able to demonstrate to the constitutional authority that their decision meets the requirements of section 1 of the Charter.

Constitutional disputes about the voting age occurred in the United States during the 1960s and 1970s. In 1970, the Supreme Court settled the issue in part in the *Oregon v. Mitchell* case, but Congress had to intervene by enacting the Twenty-sixth Amendment. It is interesting to review what took place in the United States before the right to vote at age 18 was officially enshrined in the Constitution, because it is in some respects applicable to Canada.

American Situation

The United States Supreme Court has firmly established that the right to vote is "a fundamental matter in a free and democratic society" (*Reynolds* 1964, 561). And when fundamental rights are protected by the

Equal Protection Clause of the Fourteenth Amendment, "classifications which might invade or restrain them must be closely scrutinized and carefully confined" (*Harper* 1966, 670), and "any alleged infringement of the right of citizens to vote must be carefully and meticulously scrutinized" (*Reynolds* 1964, 562).

According to the United States Constitution, the states have legislative authority to set the conditions for exercising the right to vote in both federal and local elections, but Congress may legislate the implementation of the Equal Protection Clause of the Fourteenth Amendment. That is why Congress was able to pass the *Voting Rights Act of 1965*, which was deemed to be constitutionally valid in *Katzenbach v. Morgan* (1966). It was in the 1960s and 1970s that several legislatures reduced the voting age from 21 to 18 for both federal and local elections, which created a rather embarrassing situation, particularly at the federal level. Also, in 1969, Congress decided to require the legislatures to adopt uniform standards for all elections, including the 18-year voting age rule (the Twenty-sixth Amendment).

In *Oregon v. Mitchell* (1970), the United States Supreme Court decided with a majority of five to four that setting the voting age at 18 was constitutionally valid for federal elections, but that for local elections it infringed on the autonomy of the state legislatures.

It is interesting to see the extent to which such an issue should be left to the legislators, and also the criteria that ought to obtain in determining a specified age.

Case law shows that determining the voting age involves factual considerations as well as value choices, and that these must first be dealt with by the legislators. In the *Oregon* decision, Justice Harlan wrote: "I fully agree that judgments of the sort involved here are beyond the institutional competence and constitutional authority of the judiciary ... They are pre-eminently matters for legislative discretion, with judicial review, if it exists at all, narrowly limited" (*Oregon* 1970, 206).

What Justice Douglas asks is why the line should be drawn at the age of 18 rather than of 17. Nothing prevents the legislators from deeming that young people of 18 have the maturity needed, particularly since they are "generally considered by American law to be mature enough to contract, to marry, to drive an automobile, to own a gun, and to be responsible for criminal behavior as an adult" (*Oregon* 1970, 142; judge cited Engdahl 1970, 36).

The congressional debates reveal the types of concerns that members of Congress have. The argument most often used is that of military service: "old enough to fight, old enough to vote" (Engdahl 1970, 36).[6] Nevertheless, the most important principle would appear to remain that: "all those who have a 'stake' in an election should be permitted to vote. Persons who have a significant stake in the matter affected by an election cannot be excluded from voting unless their exclusion is sufficiently important to a substantial state interest" (ibid., 37). The question is whether young people, owing to their status as workers, taxpayers and beneficiaries of government programs for college and university education, have a "stake" in elections; it should also be noted that the young people in question are allowed to join the armed forces and to participate in defending the country.

It must be recalled that in the United States, debate focused on young people in the 18- to 21-year age group. Those defending the reform (the Twenty-sixth Amendment) could easily demonstrate that the objective of the legislation was maintaining a "reasonably informed and mature" electorate (Engdahl 1970, 40). The situation would, of course, be different for those under 18 years of age. Professor Engdahl explained what the situation in the United States was during the 1970s:

> As a class, persons younger than 18 have not completed high school. They are treated as juveniles rather than adults by the criminal law, and their freedom to contract or marry is typically more restricted – all of this because the law, reflecting human experience, regards them as not yet mature enough to make balanced independent decisions. If it is relevant, their ineligibility for military service arguably gives them a lesser stake in elections. But more significant is the fact that no state has experimented with permitting persons younger than 18 to vote, so that there is a lack of evidence to refute the foregoing indications that placing the voting age lower would probably undercut the states' substantial interest in responsible republican government. (Engdahl 1970, 40)

The American experience, and the principles and attitudes that underpin it, would appear to lead to the conclusion that no change in the status quo is required, even 20 years after 1970. An effort should be made to describe the way in which Canada's position differs from that of our neighbours to the south.

Canadian Situation
The Canadian Constitution is less precise than that of the United States on the subject of the minimum age for exercising the right to vote. At the same time it asks legislators, under the control of the appropriate court, to set such an age and to indicate the criteria (those of section 1 of the Charter) to be applied more precisely.

Setting the voting age at 18 is an infringement of section 3 of the

Charter. In all of the case law bearing on this section, the courts have tended to treat even the slightest restriction to the exercise of the right to vote to be such an infringement (Garant 1991); moreover, several judges have admitted a priori that this was the case without wishing to go into greater detail on the matter, preferring instead to discuss the grounds for such a situation.

The question that has to be asked is whether setting an age at which the exercise of a right or activity can take place constitutes discrimination in itself, pursuant to the age factor considered in section 15 of the Charter. In other words, is any distinction based on age automatically to be considered "discrimination"?

The Supreme Court appears to have answered this question in the *Andrews* case (1989):

> I would say then that discrimination may be described as a distinction, whether intentional or not but based on grounds relating to personal characteristics of the individual or group, which has the effect of imposing burdens, obligations, or disadvantages on such individual or group not imposed upon others, or which withholds or limits access to opportunities, benefits, and advantages available to other members of society. Distinctions based on personal characteristics attributed to an individual solely on the basis of association with a group will rarely escape the charge of discrimination, while those based on an individual's merits and capacities will rarely be so classed. (*Andrews* 1989, 174)[7]

The Court added that, with respect to section 15 of the Charter, it was important to know whether the reason for discrimination is included in the list of grounds for non-discrimination or is analogous to the reasons in the list, whether the law treats the person or group bringing a complaint equally, whether it is applicable to such a person or group, or whether the effect of the law on it differs with respect to protection or benefits provided. It is in section 1 that possible grounds for doing so must be examined (*Andrews* 1989, 183).

In virtually all decisions bearing on age, courts of appeal and superior courts have tended to admit that any distinction based on age is an infringement of section 15 (*Stoffman* 1988; *Douglas* 1988; *Harrison* 1988; *Tétreault-Gadoury* 1989; *Sniders* 1989; *McKinney* 1990).[8] Nevertheless, one question does not appear to have been answered satisfactorily; this concerns distinctions intended to provide protection for, or to improve the situation of, a person or group. Section 15(2) states that section 15(1) does not preclude any remedial laws or programs. But ought such a law to be placed on the same footing as a law that sets the age of majority at 18, that prohibits any person under 16 years of age from driving a vehicle, that prohibits access to liquor outlets to those under 18, and so on? A number of superior court decisions have described certain statutory provisions as providing protection (*R. v. M.* 1986; *Music* 1989).

Even if it were to be admitted that legislation designed to provide protection is not discriminatory within the meaning of section 15, it would be difficult for us to consider that an elections act that prohibits persons under 18 years of age from voting should be considered as providing protection. It is not to protect young people of 17 or 16 years of age that they are prohibited from voting; there must be other reasons to explain such a prohibition.

Once it is admitted that setting the voting age at 18 constitutes an infringement of the rights recognized by sections 3 and 15 of the Charter, the grounds for doing so must be examined under section 1. Next, it must be asked whether the requirements are the same when an infringement occurs under section 3 or section 15.

In *R. v. Oakes* (1986) the Supreme Court of Canada determined what type of test ought to be applied to check compatibility with the Charter with respect to section 1. In the *R. v. Edwards Books and Art Ltd.* (1986, 768–69), it reformulated the test and gave it its definitive form (see also *Ford* 1988, 770; *Rocket* 1990, 246).

When it is established that a rule of law limits a right protected by the Charter, the government must demonstrate that the objectives of the provision are sufficiently important to justify a limitation on such a right: "First, the objective, which the measures responsible for a limit on a *Charter* right or freedom are designed to serve, must be of sufficient importance to warrant overriding a constitutionally protected right or freedom" (*Oakes* 1986, 138).

But what is meant by "of sufficient importance"? "It is necessary, at a minimum, that an objective relate to concerns which are pressing and substantial in a free and democratic society before it can be characterized as sufficiently important" (*Oakes* 1986, 139).

Once this initial step has been completed, the government must demonstrate the reasonableness of the disputed measure and justify it. There must be a degree of proportionality between the measure adopted and the desired objective. According to the Supreme Court, the proportionality criterion involves three components:

> First, the measures adopted must be carefully designed to achieve the objective in question. They must not be arbitrary, unfair or based on irrational considerations. In short, they must be rationally connected

to the objective. Second, the means, even if rationally connected to the objective in this first sense, should impair "as little as possible" the right or freedom in question: *R. v. Big M Drug Mart Ltd.* ... Third, there must be a proportionality between the effects of the measures which are responsible for limiting the *Charter* right or freedom, and the objective which has been identified as of "sufficient importance". (*Oakes* 1986, 139)

According to the Supreme Court, the more serious the infringement of the right, the more important the objective in question must be.

When the time came to apply the criteria of the *Oakes* decision to section 15 infringements, the Supreme Court appeared to be divided on what the approach ought to be of the judicial constitutional authority. According to Justices Laforest, McIntyre and Lamer, the courts should be wary, so as not to "deny the community-at-large the benefits associated with sound social and economic legislation" (*Andrews* 1989, 184).[9]

There are no Supreme Court decisions on section 3, but there is a fairly large number of cases in which other courts have explained how infringements of this fundamental right ought to be treated in light of section 1.

It is interesting to see how the Yukon Court of Appeal treated the issue in 1986, by citing the eminent American constitutional expert Tribe (1978):

Although free and open participation in the electoral process lies at the core of democratic institutions, the need to confer the franchise on all who aspire to it is tempered by the recognition that completely unlimited voting could subvert the ideal of popular rule which democracy so ardently embraces. Moreover, in deciding who may and who may not vote in its elections, a community takes a crucial step in defining its identity. If nothing else, even though anyone in the world might have some interest in any given election's outcome, a community should be empowered to exclude from its elections persons with no real nexus to the community as such. (Tribe 1978, 761)

Justice Rouleau of the Federal Court of Canada, following the lead of many others, moreover wrote: "[T]he right to vote is the cornerstone of any self-respecting democracy. Clearly then it is a right which, in my view, it is difficult to limit unless within the well-defined circumstances indicated in section 1 of the Charter" (*Lévesque* 1985, 189).

Justice Bowlby of the High Court of Ontario wrote as follows: "In a democratic society, the franchise is the very means by which the diverse views and beliefs of individuals are accommodated and through which the participation of individuals in society is achieved" (*Grondin* 1988, 430). Justice Bowlby based himself on none other than Chief Justice Dickson in the *Oakes* decision: "The Court must be guided by the values and principles essential to a free and democratic society which I believe embody ... faith in social and political institutions which enhance the participation of individuals and groups in society" (*Oakes* 1986, 136).

Justice Taylor of British Columbia is of the opinion that the right enshrined in section 3 "means more than the right to cast a ballot. It means the right to make an informed electoral choice reached through freedom of belief, conscience, opinion[,] expression, association and assembly" (*Jolivet* 1983, 434).

Justice McLachlin, in *Dixon v. British Columbia (Attorney General)*, concerning equal representation in the changing of electoral boundaries, considered that it had to be largely left to legislators and the government to adopt reasonable measures "to enact what appear to them to be reasonable measures to ensure that valid geographic and regional considerations are taken into account in establishing boundaries in the interests of better government" (1989, 276).[10]

Lastly, here is the opinion of Justice Scollin of Manitoba on the respective roles of the legislators and the courts: "The courts must beware of becoming dictators of tolerance, but in this case the lawmakers must give more considerate, as well as more vigilant, thought to the Charter implications of both the existing and any proposed new legislation" (*Badger* 1986, 164).

The choice made by federal law-makers in 1970 cannot, it is true, qualify as a measure that was adopted following in-depth study or consideration. There were three reasons why the voting age was set at 18: first, it was the age of majority in most provinces; second, most provincial statutes had adopted such a measure; third, the Twenty-sixth Amendment to the United States Constitution had just set the voting age at 18.

Now that the right to vote is enshrined in the Constitution, these arguments still hold; in our opinion, however, they are no longer sufficient. The Charter gives every citizen a constitutional right to participate in the democratic process, but this participation, which is made possible above all by means of the right to vote, must be the result of an informed process. Whenever the age limit is at issue, it is therefore essential to exclude only citizens who do not have the required maturity to vote in an informed manner. It is up to the government to demonstrate that at 17 or 16 years of age a young person does not have the maturity required to take part satisfactorily in the democratic process.

The objective of the *Canada Elections Act* on this matter, which consists of giving the right to vote only to citizens who are sufficiently mature, is clearly legitimate. It meets an important and genuine concern in society. Moreover, according to the opinion of several Supreme Court justices in recent decisions, it is difficult to question a legislative objective. Thus far, the Supreme Court has considered that the objective is sufficiently important in all cases submitted to it.[11]

An assessment of proportionality remains to be done, because the courts will have to invalidate any measure that is disproportionate to the objective.

Three Criteria in Assessing Legislative Measures

The first criterion is determining a rational link between the legislative measure and the objective. The Supreme Court has taken two approaches to the application of this criterion. The more inflexible of the two consists of making a rational link a necessity. In *R. v. Oakes* (1986, 141), the majority concluded that there was no rational link between section 8 of the *Narcotic Control Act* and the legislative objective because it would be irrational for any person found guilty of possessing a tiny quantity of drugs to be considered to have been in such possession for the purpose of trafficking. Likewise, it would be irrational to maintain that all young persons 16 or 17 years of age are incapable of satisfactorily participating in the democratic process through an informed vote.

In *R. v. Morgentaler*, Justice Beetz maintained: "A rule which is unnecessary in respect of Parliament's objectives cannot be said to be 'rationally connected' thereto" (1988, 125). And in *Ford*, the Court stated: "it has not been demonstrated that the prohibition of the use of any language other than French in ss. 58 and 59 of the *Charter of the French Language* is necessary to the defence and enhancement of the status of the French language in Quebec" (1988, 779; see also *Rocket* 1990).

In this matter, it is worth recalling that several Superior Court justices, in dealing with the removal of the right of prison inmates to vote, considered it irrational to place hardened criminals – who may perhaps be seen as having forfeited their right to take part in the democratic process – on the same footing as citizens sentenced to a few days in prison for a minor offence (Garant 1991).

In 1990, following the most recent Supreme Court decisions, the approach appeared to alternate between rigidity and greater flexibility, depending on just how fundamental the right or liberty protected was considered to be. Thus in cases where the freedom of expression on economic matters has been infringed, the Court has been more flexible

(*Rocket* 1990). On the other hand, where individual freedom and security are at issue, a stricter approach has been taken (*Martineau* 1990; *Hess* 1990, 919–22; *Reference re ss. 193 and 195.1(1)(c) of the Criminal Code (Man.)* 1990).

The second criterion is to ask whether the legislative objective is being met by the least harmful means. In some decisions, such as *Ford* (1988, 780), one may well ask whether the measure – to display advertising only in French – was necessary to meet the desired legislative objective.

In *R. v. Vaillancourt*, the Court concluded that in order to dissuade citizens from using or possessing firearms, it was not necessary to convict of murder any person who did not wish to or expect to cause death, and who could not even anticipate that such death would result (1987, 660; see also *Holmes* 1988). In *Edmonton Journal v. Alberta (Attorney General)*, Justice Cory considered that the measure at issue went far beyond the objective of protecting the privacy of individuals and thus unduly compromised the right to freedom of expression; he also added: "Any need for the protection of privacy of witnesses or children could be readily accomplished by far less sweeping measures" (1989, 1346).

Another trend that is beginning to appear in certain Court decisions, particularly because of the influence of Justice Laforest, is the need to provide legislators with sufficient latitude (*Edwards Books and Art Ltd.* 1986, 794–95; *Schwartz* 1988, 488; *United States* 1989, 1489–90). This more deferential approach is found in *Irwin Toy v. Quebec (Attorney General)* where the issue is a legislative measure designed to protect a group that is vulnerable because of its age – 13 and under. The Court, which ruled in favour of the Quebec government, stated: "This Court will not, in the name of minimal impairment, take a restrictive approach to social science evidence and require legislatures to choose the least ambitious means to protect vulnerable groups" (1989, 999).[12] This considerably attenuates the principle of minimum impairment of corporate operations. If this trend in Court decisions is applied to the legislative measure that sets the voting age at 18, the outcome will clearly be different. On 6 December 1990, the Supreme Court confirmed this approach in four decisions on compulsory retirement at age 65 (*McKinney* 1990; *Harrison* 1990; *Stoffman* 1990; *Douglas* 1990).

The third criterion regarding age consists of weighing the effects of the measure against the objective. The more important the objective, the more it can justify an infringement of the right. Chief Justice Dickson wrote in *Oakes:* "The more severe the deleterious effects of a measure, the more important the objective must be" (1986, 140); and again in *Slaight:* "a serious infringement [must be] ... only outweighed by very important objectives" (1989, 1057). Chief Justice Lamer wrote in *Reference re ss. 193 and 195.1(1)(c) of the Criminal Code (Man.):* "If the effects of the measure on individuals or groups are wholly out of proportion with the legislative objective ... the limitation cannot be one that is reasonable and demonstrably justified" (1990, 1200).

Another element to be considered in determining the proportionality between the effects and the objective is "the degree to which the measures which impose the limit trench upon the integral principles of a free and democratic society" (*Oakes* 1986, 139; see also *Reference re ss. 193 and 195.1(1)(c) of the Criminal Code (Man.)* 1990, 1200).

It is not easy to apply this criterion to our problem. On the one hand, the legislators' objective is of supreme importance: the integrity of the democratic system by means of the fullest possible participation in the electoral process. On the other hand, depriving segments of the population of the right to vote is an extremely serious infringement; legislators must have a major reason to deprive a citizen or a group of citizens of such a right. This brings us to the heart of the issue: the question of sufficient maturity to vote in an informed manner.

What then are the characteristics of "electoral maturity"? It consists of being capable of making an informed judgement on the past performance of a government and candidate, on their programs, and on their ability to fulfil an elected mandate in a satisfactory manner. To this end, it is necessary to keep informed, to take part in meetings and to dialogue with fellow citizens. A citizen who can do this has the desired electoral maturity.

How then can it be demonstrated that 17- or 16-year-olds would not have this electoral maturity? When they are legally freed from parental authority or in business, they are treated on an equal footing with adults. Otherwise, they may hold a job, pay taxes and on their own freely carry out many legal acts (they may contract and appear in court) subject to the protection conferred on them by their minor status with respect to injury. These young people, with the required consent, can marry, have family responsibilities, drive a vehicle and join the armed forces. They are criminally and civilly responsible for their actions. In Quebec at least, the law grants them collective political rights if they are enrolled in college- or university-level educational institutions.

How, in applying the criteria of the *Oakes* (1986) decision, could the government demonstrate to a court that young 17- or even 16-year-olds do not have the required electoral maturity? That some may not have it is plausible, just as it is easy to demonstrate that many adults, seniors and handicapped people do not in fact have the political maturity required to vote in an informed and meaningful manner. It is salutary to recall how American constitutional case law condemned the "literacy test" used in some American states on grounds of "equal protection."

The Supreme Court considered that legislators cannot, by imposing a test, discriminate between educated and non-educated electors. No one, moreover, has ever dreamed of making a distinction on the basis of the ability to vote in an informed manner. An objective criterion is needed to distinguish a child from an adult, and this criterion should be as far from arbitrary as possible.

It must also be recalled that the *Canada Elections Act* creates a special rule for young service personnel of less than 18 years of age that gives them the right to vote. This is discrimination with respect to those under 18 years of age who are not in service as members of the Canadian armed forces. It would be difficult to support such discrimination by applying the criteria identified in section 1 of the Charter. It cannot be doubted that young service personnel should have the right to vote. Moreover, it is interesting to note that one of the fundamental reasons why the United States Congress lowered the voting age was the "particularly unfair treatment of such citizens in view of the national defense responsibilities imposed upon such citizens" (United States, *Voting Rights Act*, s. 301a).

The Supreme Court of Canada in its four decisions of 6 December 1990 refused to invalidate the fixing of the mandatory retirement age at 65 on the grounds of equal rights (*McKinney* 1990; *Harrison* 1990; *Stoffman* 1990; *Douglas* 1990). It considered that legislators had superior objectives that overrode the infringement of rights; it was reasonable and justifiable that such discrimination with regard to age be tolerated in a free and democratic society. However, the right being infringed was assuredly not as fundamental as that of the right to vote. Moreover, it could easily be proved that, in general, young people of 17 or 16 years of age are qualified to participate in an enlightened manner in the democratic process. Thus, it can be argued that the best possible way to cause the least infringement of constitutional rights under section 3 of the Charter would be to lower the voting age. The legislative objective, which is to ensure the integrity of the democratic and electoral process, would not be compromised thereby – indeed, quite the contrary.

CONCLUSION

The arguments in favour of maintaining the voting age at 18 are impressive. The immense majority of free and democratic societies have adopted this age and no activist movements to lower it are apparent. Canadian constitutional experts appear to reject the idea out of hand (Beaudoin 1989; Gold and Cameron 1990).

The first argument that the defenders of the status quo can put forward is that in all provinces (except one), election legislation ties the voting age to the age of civil majority, which is 18. The age of majority conditions all ordinary civil legal activities. The *Criminal Code* of Canada grants important protections to those under 18 years of age, and refuses, in the law enforcement and sentencing process, to put them on the same footing with adults. In social statutes, the age of majority is clearly taken into consideration for the granting of aid or social assistance; family allowances are, under most plans, paid until the age of 18. Economic statutes, the most important of which concern business corporations, require that persons be 18 years of age to be elected to the board of directors. Legislation on the use of alcohol ties to the age of majority the right to enter liquor outlets or to buy alcohol.

Lowering the federal voting age to 17 or 16 could have an impact on all these statutes. How could one continue to regard as a minor – that is, a person whose capacity or position under the law is diminished – someone who is considered by an elections act to be a fully mature citizen?

Those in favour of lowering the voting age to 17 or 16 could respond to this first argument by noting that, in most instances, the age of majority does not in itself affect legal capacity, but rather it provides protection against injury. Legislators consider minors to be a vulnerable group requiring protection, which in fact is the function of the *Young Offenders Act*. The idea of granting protection to vulnerable groups is widespread in our system of law: law-makers thereby protect consumers, handicapped people, tenants and so on.

In social legislation, when young persons less than 18 years of age are taken into custody, is it not because legislators consider them to be "dependants"? This same legislation, however, treats differently young people who find themselves on the labour market.

By setting the age at which one can leave school at 16, legislators also implicitly consider 16-year-olds and over to be capable of entering the labour market and of working independently, which is also recognized in our labour legislation. It may be recalled that the *Civil Code of Lower Canada* grants freedom from parental authority to minors who are tradespeople or bankers. A young person 16 years of age may actively engage in economic activity in Quebec's important cooperative movement; such a person may even establish a cooperative and become a member of the board. A 16-year-old student may become a member of the board of governors of a college, or hold any other official position in the institution. Through the provincial *Act respecting the accreditation and financing of students' associations*, young Quebec college and university students are encouraged to play an active role in public life.

On a final note, legislators show confidence in young people 16 years of age by granting them the right to drive automobiles and bear firearms, two activities that involve significant risks. In addition, political parties welcome young people to their ranks, to participate actively in meetings and policy deliberations.

Linking the Legislative Measure to the Objective

The fundamental issue to be dealt with is, therefore, not to determine whether it is intrinsically reasonable to grant a voting right only to citizens 18 years of age and over, but rather to see whether the right to vote given to every citizen under the Constitution may be restricted in accordance with the criteria recognized by the Supreme Court in the *Oakes* (1986) decision. The approach taken by legislators in Canadian law can generally only provide an indication, revealing to be sure, but not sufficient to resolve the whole question.

The application of the proportionality test ought not to lead the Supreme Court to "second-guess the wisdom of policy choices made by our legislators," to cite Chief Justice Lamer (*Reference re ss. 193 and 195.1(1)(c) of the Criminal Code (Man.)* 1990, 1199). What is at issue is not whether it is wise to prohibit persons under 18 years of age from voting, but rather to determine whether the legislators' choice has been carefully designed to meet the objective, while at the same time limiting constitutional law as little as possible. It is necessary to ask whether this measure is required to meet the desired objective. Or, as Chief Justice Lamer wrote: "What is at issue then, is whether there is some reasonable alternative scheme which would allow the government to achieve its objective with fewer detrimental effects on ... freedom" (ibid., 1196).

We believe that it is difficult to see how the government would be able to demonstrate at what age it is appropriate to set the voting age to meet the legislators' objective.

The government could counter, however, that the line must be drawn somewhere! The situation is similar to the one that the Supreme Court had to deal with in *Irwin Toy* (1989). The legislators' option was based on social science evidence, on which the Court stated it would not take a "restrictive approach."

Psychological Evidence on Political Maturity

Evidence of political maturity which the government could use would come from the field of psychology. At what age has a young person reached the degree of maturity needed to possess the political or moral judgement necessary to participate satisfactorily in the democratic process?

By way of example, reference could be made to empirical research, such as that of Samson, which provides evidence that the development of moral judgement takes place in six stages. Young people generally reach the fourth stage between the ages of 16 and 20. At this stage their moral attitude "not only complies with the expectations of those around them and of the social order, but also shows loyalty to these expectations, as well as an active desire to maintain, support, and justify the social order, and to identify their views with those of the individuals and corporate entities that make it up" (1976, 18).[13] They are therefore prepared to support authority, established rules and social order. They are capable of judging what is the correct course of action, which consists of discharging their duties, being deferential toward authority and maintaining the established order.

At stage 5, individuals are capable of defining correct or morally acceptable action in terms of individual rights or in accordance with critically analysed criteria that are generally agreed upon by the whole of society.

Ideally, before being given the right to vote citizens should have reached the age of 20 and stage 5, which Samson terms "responsible awareness of the 'social compact' model." However, at stage 4, moral judgement is sufficiently well developed for the vote to be meaningful.

Questions for Law-makers and the Courts

With evidence like this from the social sciences, where certitude is often approximate, would the Supreme Court be inclined to reason as it did in *Irwin Toy* (1989)? In that case, the government showed that it is under the age of 13 that a child is vulnerable to harmful and pernicious television advertising. The Court also determined that it is constitutionally valid to prohibit commercial advertising aimed at persons less than 13 years of age, with the objective of protecting this particular population. How will the government be able to demonstrate that it is at the age of 18 that a young person reaches a stage of development sufficiently advanced to make satisfactory moral judgements? The government cannot provide evidence that it is *exactly* at age 18 that moral and political maturity are reached; all it can demonstrate is that this maturity is sufficiently developed between the ages of 16 and 20.

Why would law-makers lower the voting age from 18, to 17 or to 16? Certainly not to keep pace with a legislative movement that would generally tend to lower the age of majority or to assign weighty responsibilities or to confer rights to those under the age of 18. It is of course true that in many areas, young persons 17 or 16 years of age are granted such rights and responsibilities by our statutes, though legislators have not for that reason lowered the age of majority. All the considerations that were examined when the age of majority was lowered from 21 to 18 are easily applicable to lowering it from 18 to 17 or 16 (United

Kingdom, Parliament 1967).

It does not appear to us to be defensible, given the current state of constitutional law, to maintain that section 3 of the Charter requires that the voting age be lowered below 18, though we are not at all convinced that the Supreme Court would not invalidate fixing the voting age at 18.

Would more extensive research perhaps develop more convincing evidence? Such studies could consider the motivation of law-makers each time that a given statute might set the age at 17 or 16. They could also examine the psychology of young people of 17 or 16 years of age and formulate the most precise possible definition of the time at which they are capable of valuable moral and political judgement.

ABBREVIATIONS

B.C.S.C.	British Columbia Supreme Court
c.	chapter
C.A.	Court of Appeal
C.C.C. (3d)	Canadian Criminal Cases, Third Series
C.C.S.M.	Continuing Consolidation, Statutes of Manitoba
C.L.L.C.	Canadian Labour Law Cases
C.R.R.	Canadian Rights Reporter
D.L.R. (4th)	Dominion Law Reports, Fourth Series
Fed. T.D.	Federal Court, Trial Division
Man. Q.B.	Manitoba Court of Queen's Bench
O.R.	Ontario Reports
Pub. L.	Public Law (U.S.)
re-en.	re-enacted
R.P.	Quebec Practice Reports
R.R.Q.	Revised Regulations of Quebec
R.S.A.	Revised Statutes of Alberta
R.S.B.C.	Revised Statutes of British Columbia
R.S.C.	Revised Statutes of Canada
R.S.M.	Revised Statutes of Manitoba
R.S.N.S.	Revised Statutes of Nova Scotia
R.S.Q.	Revised Statutes of Quebec
s(s).	section(s)
S.B.C.	Statutes of British Columbia
S.C.C.	Supreme Court of Canada
S.C.R.	Supreme Court Reports
S.M.	Statutes of Manitoba
S.O.	Statutes of Ontario
S.Q.	Statutes of Quebec
U.S.	Supreme Court Reports (U.S.)

NOTES

This study was completed in August 1991.

In this study, quoted material that originated in French has been translated into English.

1. In the unpublished paper submitted to the Royal Commission on Electoral Reform and Party Financing, entitled "The Electoral Process and the Charter," Marc Gold and Jamie Cameron devote 10 lines to the matter and conclude that the determination "clearly would be upheld by the courts" (1990, 28).

2. The United States Supreme Court ruled that the *Voting Rights Act* passed by Congress was valid for congressional elections but invalid for elections to the state legislatures: it was a question of infringing on the legislative authority of the states.

3. The age of majority in British Columbia and in Nova Scotia is 19.

4. Section 31 of the *Civil Code of Lower Canada* also adds that the court may, when an application affects the interest of the child, give the child the opportunity to be heard.

5. In British Columbia, the Superintendent of Highways may dispense with the requirement for parental consent (British Columbia, *Motor Vehicle Act*, s. 28).

6. In the United States, conscription, which is often mandatory, affects persons 18 years of age and older.

7. This definition was adopted unanimously by the Court in *Turpin* (1989, 1331).

8. The *McKinney, Stoffman* and *Douglas* decisions were upheld on this point by the Supreme Court of Canada on 6 December 1990.

9. Mr. Justice Laforest added that "courts [should be] extremely wary about questioning legislative and government choices in such areas" (*Andrews* 1989, 194). The three Justices holding the majority position, Dickson, Wilson, and L'Heureux-Dubé, did not seem to share this point of view.

10. Justice McLachlin was referring to what the Supreme Court said in *R. v. Edwards Books and Art Ltd.* (1986, 713).

11. The following are legislative objectives in cases submitted to the Court: protection of family and social ties by granting a common holiday, education, the war against drug trafficking and imports, guaranteeing of essential services, reduction of inflation, economic loss suffered by milk producers, deterrence of the use of firearms in committing offences, protection of the fetus, highway safety, detection and identification of highway safety offences, identification of drivers whose faculties are weakened

(and the deterrent effect thereof), elimination of residential burglary, protection of the public against drunk drivers, protection of children by discouraging males from having sexual relations with girls under 14 years of age, law enforcement and improved administration of justice, unimpeded access to courts, protection of the French language, regulation and control of the legal profession, measures to counter uneven relations between employers and employees, protection of groups susceptible to the powers of advertising, bringing of criminals to trial and enforcement of the law even beyond national boundaries, protection of privacy for individuals during marital proceedings, obtaining of public support for the criminal trial process, elimination of problems related to the nuisance caused by soliciting in the streets.

12. The Quebec law being challenged forbade commercial advertising geared to young people aged 13 and under.

13. Other contemporary research by specialists in this discipline could be cited to demonstrate that moral judgement is already sufficiently developed at age 16.

BIBLIOGRAPHY

Alberta. *Alberta Income Tax Act*, R.S.A. 1980, c. A-31, s. 10.

————. *Co-operative Associations Act*, R.S.A. 1980, c. C-24.

————. *Employment Pension Plans Act*, R.S.A. 1980, c. E-10.05.

————. *Fire Prevention Act*, R.S.A. 1980, c. F-10.1, s. 12.

————. *Insurance Act*, R.S.A. 1980, c. I-5, s. 364.

————. *International Child Abduction Act*, R.S.A. 1980, c. I-6.5.

————. *Maintenance and Recovery Act*, R.S.A. 1980, c. M-2.

————. *Maintenance Order Act*, R.S.A. 1980, c. M-1.

————. *Manpower Development Act*, R.S.A. 1980, c. M-3.

————. *Marriage Act*, R.S.A. 1980, c. M-6.

————. *Provincial Courts Act*, R.S.A. 1980, c. P-20, s. 42.

————. *Wildlife Act*, R.S.A. 1980, c. W-9.1.

————. *Women's Institute Act*, R.S.A. 1980, c. W-13.

Andrews v. Law Society (B.C.), [1989] 1 S.C.R. 143.

Badger v. Manitoba (Attorney General) (1986), 27 C.C.C. (3d) 158 (Man. Q.B.).

Beaudoin, Gérald A. 1989. "Democratic Rights." In *The Canadian Charter of Rights and Freedoms*. 2d ed., ed. G-A. Beaudoin and E. Ratushny. Toronto: Carswell.

Boyer, J. Patrick. 1981. *Political Rights, the Legal Framework of Elections in Canada*. Toronto: Butterworths.

British Columbia. *Accountants (Management) Act*, R.S.B.C. 1979, c. 3, s. 4.

———. *Family and Child Service Act*, S.B.C. 1980, c. 11.

———. *Fisheries Act*, R.S.B.C. 1979, c. 137, s. 8.

———. *Infants Act*, R.S.B.C. 1979, c. 196, s. 16.

———. *Insurance Act*, R.S.B.C. 1979, c. 200.

———. *Land Title Act*, R.S.B.C. 1979, c. 219.

———. *Mental Health Act*, R.S.B.C. 1979, c. 256, s. 19.

———. *Motor Vehicle Act*, R.S.B.C. 1979, c. 288, s. 28.

———. *Municipal Act*, R.S.B.C. 1979, c. 290, s. 513.

———. *Pawnbrokers Act*, R.S.B.C. 1979, c. 314.

———. *Small Claims Act*, R.S.B.C. 1979, c. 387.

———. *Weed Control Act*, R.S.B.C. 1979, c. 432.

———. *Wildlife Act*, R.S.B.C. 1979, c. 433.

British Columbia. Royal Commission on Electoral Reform. 1978. *Report*, vol. 14. Victoria, BC.

Canada. *Canada Business Corporations Act*, R.S.C. 1985, c. C-44.

———. *Canada Elections Act*, R.S.C. 1985, c. E-2, Sched. II, s. 21.

———. *Criminal Code*, R.S.C. 1985, c. C-46, ss. 13, 148, 171–72, 212, 215.

———. *Canadian Charter of Rights and Freedoms*, ss. 1–3, 15, 32, Part I of the *Constitution Act, 1982*, being Schedule B of the *Canada Act 1982* (U.K.), c. 11.

———. *Family Allowances Act*, R.S.C. 1985, c. F-1, s. 3.

———. *Narcotic Control Act*, R.S.C. 1970, c. N-1, s. 8.

———. *National Defence Act*, R.S.C. 1985, c. N-5, s. 20.

———. *Young Offenders Act*, R.S.C. 1985, c. Y-1, ss. 16, 20, 24.1.

Canada. House of Commons. 1969–70. *Debates*. Index, "Voting Age."

Canada. House of Commons. Standing Committee on Privileges and Elections. 1970. *Hearings*, Vol. 28, 17 February. Ottawa: Queen's Printer.

Dixon v. British Columbia (Attorney General) (1989), 59 D.L.R. (4th) 247 (B.C.S.C.).

Douglas/Kwantlen Faculty Assn. v. Douglas College (1988), 49 D.L.R. (4th) 749 (C.A.); affirmed (1990), 77 D.L.R. (4th) 94 (S.C.C.).

Edmonton Journal v. Alberta (Attorney General), [1989] 2 S.C.R. 1326.

"Eighteen Year Old Case: The Power of Congress to Legislate under the Fourteenth Amendment." 1971. *Missouri Law Review* 4:1–18.

"The Eighteen-Year-Old Vote – A Franchise Extended." 1971. *New York Law Review* 17:614–28.

Engdahl, D.E. 1970. "Constitutionality of the Voting Age Statute." *George Washington Law Review* 39:1–41.

Ford v. *Quebec (Attorney General),* [1988] 2 S.C.R. 712.

Forkosch, M.D. 1970. "Inability of Congress to Impinge on State Power to Set Electoral Age Qualifications." *Chicago-Kent Law Review* 47:1–14.

Garant, Patrice. 1991. "La Charte constitutionnelle de 1982 et la démocratie électorale canadienne." *Revue française de Droit constitutionnel* 5:1–34.

Gold, Marc, and Jamie Cameron. 1990. "The Electoral Process and the Charter." Paper prepared for the Royal Commission on Electoral Reform and Party Financing. Ottawa.

Grondin v. *Ontario (Attorney General)* (1988), 65 O.R. (2d) 427 (H.C.).

Harper v. *Virginia State Board of Elections* 383 U.S. 663 (1966).

Harrison v. *University of British Columbia* (1988), 49 D.L.R. (4th) 687 (C.A.).

Irwin Toy v. *Quebec (Attorney General),* [1989] 1 S.C.R. 927.

Jolivet v. *Canada* (1983), 7 C.C.C. (3d) 431 (B.C.S.C.).

Katzenbach v. *Morgan* 384 U.S. 641 (1966).

Lévesque v. *Canada (Attorney General)* (1985), 25 D.L.R. (4th) 184 (Fed. T.D.).

Manitoba. *Child and Family Services Act,* R.S.M. 1987, c. C80, s. 108.

———. *Credit Unions Act,* R.S.M. 1987, c. C300; repealed S.M. 1970, c. 53, s. 179.

———. *Credit Unions Act,* S.M. 1970, c. 53; repealed S.M. 1977, c. 51, s. 199.

———. *Credit Unions and Caisses Populaires Act,* S.M. 1977, c. 51, s. 56.

———. *Income Tax Act,* R.S.M. 1987, c. I10, s. 4.1.

McInnis v. *Halifax (City) Social Planning Dept., Director* (1990) 70 D.L.R. (4th) 296 (N.S.C.A.).

McKinney v. *University of Guelph* (1988), 63 O.R. (2d) 1 (Ont. C.A.); affirmed (1990), 91 C.L.L.C. 17, 004 (S.C.C.).

Music Explosion v. *Parkin,* Man. Q.B, 15 December 1989.

Nova Scotia. *Children's Services Act,* R.S.N.S. 1987, c. 68.

———. *Family Maintenance Act,* R.S.N.S. 1989, c. 160.

———. *Student Aid Act,* R.S.N.S. 1989, c. 449.

Nowak, J.E., R.D. Rotunda and J.N. Young. 1986. *Constitutional Law*. 3d ed. St. Paul, Minn.: West Publishing.

Ontario. *Child and Family Services Act, 1984*, S.O. 1984, c. 55, ss. 31, 63; re-en. S.O. 1989, c. 56, s. 2.

Oregon v. Mitchell 400 U.S. 112 (1970).

Qualter, Terence H. 1970. *The Election Process in Canada*. Toronto: McGraw-Hill.

Quebec. *Accreditation and financing of students' associations, An Act respecting*, R.S.Q. c. A-3.01.

——. *Building contractors vocational qualifications, An Act respecting*, R.S.Q. c. Q-1, s. 32.

——. *Change of name and of other particulars of civil status, An Act respecting the*, R.S.Q. c. C-10.

——. *Civil Code of Lower Canada*, arts. 20, 21, 31, 115–19, 314, 315, 987, 1001.

——. *Civil Code of Quebec*, arts. 402, 403, 429, 598, 602, 606, 646, 650, 651, 653, 654.

——. *Code of Civil Procedure*, R.S.Q. c. C-25, art. 56.

——. *Companies Act*, R.S.Q. c. C-38, s. 123.73.

——. *Co-operatives Act*, R.S.Q. c. C-67.2.

——. *Election Act*, S.Q. 1978, c. 6.

——. *Election Act*, R.S.Q. c. E-3.3

——. *Family assistance allowances, An Act respecting*, R.S.Q. c. A-17.

——. *General and Vocational Colleges Act*, R.S.Q. c. C-29.

——. *Highway Code*, R.S.Q. c. C-24.

——. *Highway Safety Code*, R.S.Q. c. C-24.2.

——. *Industrial accidents and occupational diseases, An Act respecting*, R.S.Q. c. A-3.001.

——. *Labour Code*, R.S.Q. c. C-27.

——. *Labour standards, An Act respecting*, R.S.Q. c. N-1.1

——. *Referendum Act*, R.S.Q. c. C-64.1.

——. *Regulation respecting the application of the Real Estate Brokerage Act*, R.R.Q. 1981, c. C-73, r. 1.

——. *Youth Protection Act*, R.S.Q. c. P-34.1, ss. 1, 2, 46, 52, 53.1, 54.

Quebec. Assemblée nationale. 1978. *Débats*. 12 June.

——. *Débats*. 19 December.

Quebec. Chief Electoral Officer. 1983. *Statutory Report*. Quebec.

R. v. Edwards Books and Art Ltd., [1986] 2 S.C.R. 713.

R. v. Hess, [1990] 2 S.C.R. 906.

R. v. Holmes, [1988] 1 S.C.R. 914.

R. v. M. (1986), 19 C.R.R. 179 (Man. Q.B.).

R. v. Martineau, [1990] 2 S.C.R. 633.

R. v. Morgentaler, [1988] 1 S.C.R. 30.

R. v. Oakes, [1986] 1 S.C.R. 103.

R. v. Schwartz, [1988] 2 S.C.R. 443.

R. v. Turpin, [1989] 1 S.C.R. 1296.

R. v. Vaillancourt, [1987] 2 S.C.R. 636.

Reference re ss. 193 and 195.1(1)(c) of the Criminal Code (Man.), [1990] 1 S.C.R. 1123.

Reynolds v. Sims 377 U.S. 533 (1964).

Rimouski Ready Mix Inc. v. Beaulieu, [1981] R.P. 330 (C.A.).

Rocket v. Royal College of Dental Surgeons (Ont.), [1990] 2 S.C.R. 232.

Samson, Jean-Marc. 1976. "L'éthique, l'éducation et le développement du jugement moral." In *Le développement moral*. Montreal: Fides.

Slaight Communication v. Davidson, [1989] 1 S.C.R. 1038.

Sniders v. Nova Scotia (Attorney General) (1989), 55 D.L.R. (4th) 408 (C.A.).

Stoffman v. Vancouver General Hospital (1988), 49 D.L.R. (4th) 727 (C.A.); affirmed (1990), 91 C.L.L.C. 17, 003 (S.C.C.).

Stone, G.R., L.M. Seidman, C.R. Sunstein and M.V. Tushnet. 1986. *Constitutional Law*. Boston: Little, Brown.

Tancelin, Maurice. 1988. *Des obligations: contrat et responsabilité*. 4th ed. Montreal: Wilson & Lafleur.

Tétreault-Gadoury v. Canada (Employment and Immigration Commission), [1989] 2 F.C. 245 (C.A.); reversed (1991), 91 C.L.L.C. 14, 023 (S.C.C.).

Tribe, Laurence H. 1978. *American Constitutional Law*. Mineola: Foundation Press.

United Kingdom. *Constitution Act, 1867*, 30 & 31 Vict., c. 3, s. 92.

United Kingdom. Parliament. Committee on the Age of Majority. 1967. *Report*. Cmnd. 3382. London: H.M.S.O.

United States. *Constitution of the United States*, 1788.

————. *Fourteenth Amendment*, 1868.

————. *Twenty-Sixth Amendment*, 1971.

————. *Voting Rights Act of 1965*, Pub. L. 89-110, Aug. 6, 1965, 79 Stat. 437 (Title 42, 1971, 1973–1973p).

————. *Voting Rights Amendment of 1970*, Pub. L. 91-285, June 22, 1970, 84 Stat. 314, 315 (Title 42, 1973note, 1973b, 1973c, 1973aa-1973bb-4), s. 301 (a).

United States v. Cotroni, [1989] 1 S.C.R. 1469.

Yukon Election Residency Requirement, Re (1986), 27 D.L.R. (4th) 146 (Yukon C.A.).

3

LOWERING THE VOTING AGE TO 16

~

Jon H. Pammett
John Myles

LOWERING THE VOTING AGE TO 18 YEARS

IN THE SPEECH from the Throne delivered on 23 October 1969, the federal government announced its intention of introducing a bill to lower the voting age to 18 years. The Speech explained in the following manner that the proposed action was being undertaken on the grounds of public demand, particularly from those in the relevant 18–21 age group.

> A disturbing element in many countries of the world has been the rising tide of unrest, particularly among young people. It has expressed itself in many ways, in public debate, in peaceful protest and sometimes in violence. Our profound disapproval of the excesses must not blind us to deeply felt and legitimate aspirations. Many citizens in our own country believe that they are entitled to assume greater responsibility for the destiny of our society. Such demands, insofar as they do not conflict with the general welfare, are the expression of a truly democratic ideal. They must be satisfied if our society is to attain its goals of peace and justice.
>
> The Government believes that the time has come to extend the franchise in federal elections and it will therefore recommend to the Standing Committee on Privileges and Elections of the House of Commons that the voting age be lowered to eighteen. (Canada, House of Commons 1969, 2)

The idea of lowering the voting age to 18 years was by no means a radical notion in 1969. The United Kingdom had adopted the voting age of 18 in 1968. The change was imminent in many other countries;

for example, the move to 18 was made in Germany in 1970 and in United States federal elections in 1971.[1] Moreover, seven of the Canadian provinces had lowered the voting age below 21 years by this time, with Saskatchewan, Manitoba, Prince Edward Island and Quebec standing at 18 years, and British Columbia, Alberta and Newfoundland at 19 years.

Newspaper commentary on the proposed measure was generally supportive; for example, the editorials in the *Globe and Mail*, the *Winnipeg Free Press* and the *Ottawa Citizen* all praised the move the next day. The parliamentary debate was quiet and acquiescent (Canada, House of Commons 1970). The only point of substantive dispute was whether the age of political candidacy should also be reduced to 18 years, as it subsequently was. The parliamentary committee to which the legislation had been referred had recommended against this aspect of the change, a recommendation ignored by the government when drafting the bill. As a result of the change, legal "age of majority" laws were adjusted in the provinces, establishing 18 years as the age at which individuals could legally enter into contracts.

Whereas élite opinion was virtually unanimous in favouring the lowering of the voting age to 18 years in 1970, the mass public was much more ambivalent about the matter. Table 3.1 shows the distribution of public opinion in Gallup polls between 1945 and late 1969 on the question: "In a federal election, people can't vote until they are 21. It has been suggested that persons 18, 19 and 20 years old be allowed to vote. Would you approve or disapprove if this were done?"

Table 3.1 shows that immediate postwar opinion was evenly divided on the question of allowing 18-year-olds to vote, but a trend of overall public disapproval quickly set in and persisted until the 1960s. No Gallup polls were done on this question between 1958 and 1966, so it is impossible to know when opinion swung back to the more even

Table 3.1
Public opinion on lowering the voting age to 18 years, 1945–69
(percentages)

	1945	1947	1952	1954	1958	1966	1968	1969
Approve	47	43	39	39	35	48	56	50
Disapprove	47	50	55	46	53	46	38	44
Don't know/no answer	6	7	6	15	12	6	6	6

Sources: Gallup poll press releases and *Gallup Reports* for 10 January 1953, 22 November 1958, 24 August 1968, 14 June 1969 and 31 January 1970.

division seen on the latter date. By 1968, public opinion in support of the change had reached its highest point, which was, however, only 56 percent support. It is interesting to note that a poll taken at the end of 1969, after the new policy was announced in the Speech from the Throne, showed that the public had "cooled off" (Gallup's words) on the question of lowering the voting age.[2]

If public opinion in general could at best be described as "mildly supportive" of the policy of lowering the voting age to 18 in the late 1960s, what about the "restless youth" that the Throne Speech maintains was "demanding" to be allowed to exercise its democratic responsibility? The Gallup polls cited above contain no measure of restlessness; neither do they sample the 18–20-year-old group. However, table 3.2 reveals that the relationship of age to approval of the change is not very strong among the adult population. The only finding of much substance in table 3.2 is the consistent tendency of the oldest age group (50 years and over) to be less enamoured with the change.

On two occasions, 1958 and 1968, the Gallup poll asked respondents, in an open-ended manner, to give their reasons for supporting or opposing lowering the voting age to 18 years. These reasons are instructive and are summarized in table 3.3.

There were essentially three reasons advanced for lowering the voting age to 18. Most commonly mentioned, in both years, was the fact that young people between the ages of 18 and 21 were legally permitted to do other "citizen activities" such as fighting for their country in the armed forces, earning a living and paying taxes, getting married and driving automobiles. The second argument is based on a different premise, that of knowledge or maturity – young people, it was argued, were becoming "mature enough to vote" at younger ages than in earlier times. The third reason is different yet again; it is based on the premise that the way to involve young people in political affairs

Table 3.2

Approval of lowering the voting age to 18 years by age group, 1968 and 1969
(percentages)

	National	21 – 29 yrs.	30 – 39 yrs.	40 – 49 yrs.	50+
1968 approve	56	61	59	58	49
1969 approve	50	53	53	58	39

Sources: Gallup poll press releases and *Gallup Reports* for 10 January 1953, 22 November 1958, 24 August 1968, 14 June 1969 and 31 January 1970.

Table 3.3
Reasons for supporting or opposing lowering the voting age to 18 years, 1958 and 1968
(percentages)

In support	
1958	
Old enough to do other things: go to war, work, pay taxes, get married, etc.	60
Mature before 21 nowadays; better educated	21
Would promote responsibility; encourage them to learn about politics, voice their opinions	21
1968	
Old enough to do other things: marriage, work, pay taxes, drive cars, fight for country	41
Better educated today; well informed; interested	23
Responsibility good for them; help them grow up; have voice in their own affairs	15
In opposition	
1958	
They are immature until 21	38
They lack the qualifications; not taxpayers; no stake in the country	26
They are irresponsible; too easily swayed; vote as their parents vote; can't make decisions	26
1968	
Immature; uninformed; uninterested; not wise enough	42
Not responsible; lack stability; easily influenced; inexperienced; undisciplined; lack judgement	42

Sources: Gallup poll press releases and *Gallup Reports* for 22 November 1958 and 24 August 1968.

and encourage good citizenship is to give them the responsibility to act as full voting members of the community. All three of these arguments, it will be seen, are relevant to the proposal to lower the voting age below 18.

Similarly, the reasons given for opposing the lowering of the voting age to 18 have resonance in the current debate over lowering the age even further. Most commonly, those opposed cited the "immaturity" of young people as a reason for not trusting them with the franchise. In a related argument, others opposed to the change cited the alleged inability of young people to make their own decisions and felt they would be too easily influenced by their parents or by others. Finally, the 1958 survey turned up an argument that young people did not have enough of a stake in the community, in terms of paying taxes or other citizen responsibilities. The maturity, responsibility, independence and knowledge of 16- and 17-year-olds are questions currently before us, as are questions about the effect of lowering the voting age to 16 on the legal age for general civic responsibility.

VOTER TURNOUT AND ATTITUDES OF AGE GROUPS

Studies have usually shown that, since their enfranchisement in Canada for the 1972 federal election, 18–20-year-olds have voted at lower rates than other age groups in the population. In a study on voting turnout prepared separately for the Royal Commission on Electoral Reform, Pammett (1991) used a large pooled Gallup poll sample relating to the 1984 federal election and showed that the reported voting turnout rate of 18–21-year-olds was 63 percent. The turnout rate rose to 71 percent among 22–29-year-olds, and varied between 83 and 88 percent for older age groups.

The voting turnout rate among respondents to the Canadian National Election Surveys (CNES) conducted since 1965 is more variable among age groups, but does at times show the youngest age group reporting voting at lesser rates (table 3.4). Since there was no CNES in 1972, the first study in which one can measure the effects of the reform is that for 1974 (Clarke et al. 1991, xii). One can see from table 3.4 that there is in fact no difference in turnout rate between the 18–20-year-old group and those aged 21–25; both groups, however, reported voting at lower rates than older age groups. Other patterns are evident for other years in the CNES sequence. For the elections of 1979 and 1984, the 18–20-year-old voters have the lowest turnout rate in the surveys; however, for 1980 and 1988, the youngest age group actually reports voting at a slightly higher rate than the 21–25-year-olds. Turnout rates for all groups in table 3.4 are overestimates, both because non-voters are less likely to participate in surveys and because some non-voting respondents report voting. Our interest here, however, is in the differential turnout rate between age groups, and there is no reason to believe that

Table 3.4
Voting turnout rate by age group, Canadian National Election Surveys, 1965–88
(percentages)

Age	1965	1968	1974	1979	1980	1984	1988
18–20	—	—	73	79	87	67	82
21–25	81	80	73	88	82	75	79
26–35	82	82	80	90	88	85	87
36–45	90	90	81	94	91	90	91
46–55	88	89	88	92	93	91	93
56–65	90	87	87	93	89	89	95
66+	88	82	84	87	84	90	96

this is distorted. Persons aged 18, 19 and 20 years at times vote at lower rates than older citizens, but a majority of them do vote.

Just as voting rates of the youngest age group are not dramatically different from the rest of the electorate, neither did the enfranchisement of this group produce new political alignments or work to the benefit of any one political party over long periods of time. There has in fact been a tendency for newly eligible voters entering the electorate to cast their first vote "conservatively," that is, to disproportionately favour the party already in power. Thus, newly eligible voters gave pluralities of their support to the Conservatives in 1988 and the Liberals in 1974 and 1979. In the Conservative landslide victory of 1984, new voters behaved very similarly to the rest of the electorate in favouring that party (Clarke et al. 1991, 131–35).

A number of political attitudes of age groups in Canada can be investigated from the National Election Surveys, and are displayed in table 3.5. Persons 18–20 years old are in general not substantially different in these attitudes from the next oldest group, those 21–25 years. In many ways, it makes sense to talk about "under 25" as a group, rather than to single out those between 18 and 21. In the absence of

Table 3.5
Political attitudes of age groups, Canadian National Election Surveys, 1974, 1984
(percentages)

Age	18–20	21–25	26–35	36–45	46–55	56–65	66+
(a) Interest in politics generally ("very" or "fairly" interested)							
1974	44	45	54	58	66	66	65
1984	38	45	56	66	72	74	73
(b) Interest in the election ("very" or "fairly" interested)							
1974	52	55	67	69	73	75	73
1984	58	65	67	74	83	78	75
(c) So many others vote in federal elections that it doesn't really matter whether I vote or not (agree)							
1974	16	12	9	18	14	13	24
1984	29	20	20	16	14	18	19
(d) People like me have no say in what the government does (agree)							
1974	48	50	48	54	56	64	64
1984	59	66	61	60	62	70	72
(e) Government does not care what people like me think (agree)							
1984	53	57	64	63	67	71	66
(f) Government wastes a lot of money they collect in taxes ("strongly agree")							
1984	37	39	46	51	54	57	60

data on the political attitudes of those 16 and 17 years old, it is reasonable to expect them to be similar to those in table 3.5 who appear in the 18–20 and the 21–25 groups.

Two things stand out as contrasts between the youngest and older groups, particularly groups of those who are much older. First, young people are less interested, both in politics generally (category a) and in the particular election under consideration (category b). The differences between young and old are much more substantial with regard to general political interest than with election interest. Thus, category b of table 3.5 shows that, in 1984, 58 percent of 18–20-year-olds, and 65 percent of 21–25-year-olds were at least "fairly interested" in the election, compared with the peak of 83 percent of 46–55-year-olds who were similarly interested. It is well known that political interest and participation peak among those in their 40s and 50s, since people of those ages are more likely to feel they have come to understand the political world, are personally affected by government policies, and have the time to participate or pursue their interest (Mishler 1979; Milbrath 1965).

We expect that 16- and 17-year-olds would be slightly lower in general political interest and election interest than the youngest age groups shown in table 3.5. With regard to any specific election, it is likely that around half of the 16–17-year-old age group would be at least "fairly interested" in the election. Given the voting rates of the different age groups, it is also reasonable to expect that at least half, and perhaps as many as 60 percent, of this age group would vote in federal elections if given the opportunity. This conclusion is buttressed by category c of table 3.5, which reports the answers of the CNES respondents to the question of whether they feel that so many other people vote in elections that it doesn't matter whether they vote or not. Relatively small numbers of Canadians agree with this proposition, including minorities of those in younger age groups. We expect that, if the franchise were extended to 16- and 17-year-olds, a majority of persons of these ages would also consider that their votes "count."

The other difference between young and older age groups in table 3.5 has to do with feelings of cynicism, "alienation," and political efficacy (the feeling that one can have an influence on the political process). In general, young people are less cynical about politics and have higher feelings of political efficacy than do older people. Categories d, e and f of table 3.5 show that substantially fewer 18–20-year-olds than 46–55-year-olds feel that they have no say in what the government does, that government does not care what they think, or that government wastes a lot of tax money.

Extrapolating again from these findings to the 16- and 17-year-old population, we expect to find this group to be lower in political cynicism than older age groups, more trusting in the intentions of those in government, and more likely to believe that their activities can make a difference in influencing government policy. Younger persons are somewhat more "idealistic" than older ones. One argument for lowering the voting age is based on the premise that beginning to involve young people as citizens is desirable in order to sustain their beliefs that their participation is valued and will make a difference. If young people are encouraged to begin their political participation at ages when they believe this participation will "count," it is possible that this belief may be sustained into the adult years and that the whole belief structure of Canadian society may shift in a more participatory direction.

THE ARGUMENTS PRO AND CON

As part of our investigation we examined the reasons for and against changing the voting age advanced by witnesses who appeared before the Commission and given in briefs submitted to it. We also met with students and teachers at two Ottawa high schools to get their views on whether the voting age should be lowered. None of these sources is necessarily "representative" of the Canadian population or young Canadians. Although this is an obstacle to identifying the exact distribution of public opinion on the matter, we were quickly able to identify the main arguments and the logic underlying them. There is a set of recurring themes that emerged from the briefs, witness statements and our discussions with students and teachers. These in many ways echo the views and opinions expressed in earlier debates over lowering the voting age from 21 to 18 years.

The main arguments are of two types: procedural and substantive. Procedural arguments typically point to the arbitrary character of any age-based entitlement or to inconsistencies of application. Substantive arguments appeal to negative or positive consequences that might follow from a change in the voting age.

Procedural arguments point to the fact that any age-based entitlement is by definition arbitrary. Using chronological age to restrict access to jobs (as with retirement rules), the political process or the use of alcohol or automobiles is a form of "statistical discrimination" against individuals that is usually justified in terms of the collective good. We exclude categories of people from certain rights or privileges, not because we believe all such persons are incompetent or will abuse that right, but because we believe the *risk* or *probability* of incompetence or abuse is unacceptably high. The most common argument among those who favour retaining current practice takes this form. In their view, younger persons are less likely to have the knowledge, motivation and maturity to make informed, responsible electoral decisions. They are, it is sometimes argued, more susceptible to peer pressure, fads and "single-issue" politics. In response, those who favour lowering the voting age point out that age is no guarantee of knowledge, motivation or maturity. Many high school students are no doubt better informed on current political events than many adults, who may also be influenced by peer pressure or single-issue campaigns.

There are several dimensions to this argument. As in the case of obligatory retirement, some persons object to any use of statistical discrimination to limit individual rights. Reference is made to the *Canadian Charter of Rights and Freedoms*, which prohibits discrimination on the basis of age. Other persons, who do not object to statistical discrimination in principle (e.g., for access to alcohol), question the risk involved and the criteria of risk. Is the difference between 16-year-olds and 25-year-olds sufficient to warrant exclusion of the former from the electoral process? How would one measure this risk and establish criteria for "acceptability"? What is the distribution of risk among various age groups? Should the burden of proof fall on those who want to maintain current practice or on those who would change it? A report prepared for the Royal Commission (Garant 1991) takes the view that the case for restricting the voting age to 18 might not persuade the courts if a case were brought before them based on the equality provisions of the *Canadian Charter of Rights and Freedoms*.

A second set of procedural arguments is concerned with the inconsistency of the application of current age-based entitlements. At 16 years, young people can currently leave school, leave home, marry, enter the work force and pay income taxes. We found the principle of "no taxation without representation" to be a common objection to the current practice of denying 16- and 17-year-olds the vote. The taxation referred to is primarily that resulting from full-time employment, as taxes of many sorts are of course paid by anyone of any age who buys anything.

Substantive arguments have to do with the desirable or undesirable consequences imputed to a change in the voting age. One brief to the Commission was concerned that lowering the voting age would create a political constituency that would demand (and get) a corresponding reduction in the legal drinking age, a move that was seen as having undesirable consequences. In our discussions with students, a common theme was that a reduction in the drinking age would not be desirable, and it was not presumed to follow from a lowering of the voting age.

A major substantive objective among those who favour lowering the voting age is to improve the effectiveness of political education in Canada by involving young people in the political process while most of them are still in school. Thus, a survey study conducted for the Royal Commission (Hudon et al. 1991) argues that, despite the fact that a majority of their sample of students was not in favour of lowering the voting age, such a change would encourage young people to become engaged with a political system they now regard as distant and uninteresting.

Many witnesses before the Commission, and many people to whom we spoke, complained about the lack of understanding of Canadian politics and the Canadian electoral system not only among young people but also among adults. This they attributed to a failure of the education system. Despite the fact that the curriculum provides a certain amount of direct content about the political system (see below), this is not seen as having practical importance to young people who are currently prevented from participating in elections. As the Chief Electoral Officer of Newfoundland, who supported in his brief the lowering of the voting age to 16, observed: "Because students in high schools would be eligible voters, the school system would be drawn into the democratic electoral process in a *practical* way whenever elections are called." At present, he records, what is learned is learned only at the level of theory.

With this, the debate comes full circle. Those who favour keeping the voting age at 18 years point to the lack of knowledge, motivation and maturity of younger age groups. Those who favour lowering the voting age see this reform as the solution: by involving young people and the school system in the electoral process, over time a better educated and more informed citizenry will develop.

CIVICS EDUCATION IN THE SCHOOLS

With consideration of the addition of 16- and 17-year-olds to the electoral rolls comes naturally the question of whether the high schools currently give students of that age the basic training that would enable them to vote knowledgeably. Table 3.3 showed that the amount of information, knowledge and interest possessed by young people is an important component of popular attitudes toward the advisability of giving them citizen rights and duties. Without a full-scale survey of the political knowledge and attitudes of 16- and 17-year-olds, it is impossible to document existing knowledge levels. In addition, it is worth noting that demonstrations of political knowledge and sophistication are not required of older adult voters. One does know, however, that some "civics education" does take place in high schools.

The appendix provides a detailed tabulation of courses relating to civics provided in elementary and high schools in all provinces and territories. The following discussion incorporates examples from the appendix.

In the history course that is compulsory in Ontario for grade 10 (in some places, grade 9) students, there is a nine-week unit on "Citizenship: Government and Law." About 60 percent of Ontario high school students take the "advanced" version of this course, 30 percent the "intermediate," and the remaining 10 percent the "basic." This course, with varying levels of complexity, goes through the steps involved in organizing federal elections, including the calling of an election, candidate selection, enumeration and voting procedures, and the functions of the chief electoral officer and returning officers.

A number of learning aids are available to teachers for this portion of the grade 10 history course. There is a film-strip entitled *How Canadian Government Works*. An activity suggested in the course guide provided by the Ottawa Board of Education is an election exercise with a classroom polling station. Guidance is given in decision-making skills (indeed, decision making is a focus in many parts of the high school curriculum) and their application to evaluating the relative merits of party policies, leaders and local candidates in a federal election. There are a number of impressive new textbooks keyed directly to this component of the course (for example, Ricker and Saywell 1991). In this and other courses in today's high schools, an attempt is made to give students instruction in "media literacy," including the effects of television and other media on the electoral process. Students are encouraged to look analytically, and with scepticism, on the media presentation of political and other images.

In Ontario, then, at the grade 10 (or 9) level, when students are turning 16, they are given a direct dose of "civics education" on a number of subjects, including the conduct of Canadian federal elections. It might be argued that such education would have more impact if the learning of this material had the immediacy of training young people for their participation in an election that might involve them at ages 16 or 17, rather than years later. As it is now, they are being prepared in grades 9 or 10 for something that might not take place for four or more years, their actual opportunity to cast a first ballot.

The Ontario high school system offers as well an optional upper-level course in politics. This course is designed to prepare students for university courses in the social sciences. Its outline reads like a rudimentary course in political science. Ministry of Education officials believe that this course is reasonably widely available, but have no statistics on enrolment.

The situation in many other provinces appears similar to that in Ontario. The western provinces, comments one expert, "give adequate attention to the teaching of politics" in their school curricula (Osborne 1988). He elaborates: "One may quarrel with the way in which particular units are organized or material is presented, but the subject is certainly not ignored. In general terms, these aspects of politics are included in all curricula: political institutions; the constitution; the structure of government at federal, provincial and municipal levels; law; contemporary problems; human rights; citizenship; multiculturalism; and individual rights and responsibilities. Throughout, the emphasis is upon the importance of informed, responsible, participant citizenship" (ibid., 79). In Alberta and British Columbia, civics education starts at the grade 6 level and continues into high school. There are also a number of elective courses. Manitoba has compulsory courses with civics components in grades 9 and 10.

The situation in the eastern provinces is less comprehensive when it comes to political education. With the exception of Newfoundland, there are no compulsory high school courses that give political knowledge in any of the Atlantic provinces. Nova Scotia and New Brunswick introduce some rudimentary political material in elementary school. In New Brunswick, a Canadian and comparative government course is offered in 10 of 50 schools for a total enrolment of 350 students. In Prince Edward Island, a grade 10 course that includes education in the structures of Canadian government has 310 students enrolled; a grade 11 course on Canada's political system picks up another 139 students. In Nova Scotia, the grade 12 curriculum includes a political science course taken by less than two percent of the students. In all three provinces, some instruction in the basic forms of Canadian government, including elections, is part of the history curriculum (Conley 1988). The Quebec situation appears similar to that in the Atlantic provinces; little explicit instruction is called for in the compulsory curriculum, but many teachers seek to give instruction in the basics of voting (Mercier 1988).

We have catalogued here (and more fully in the appendix) the civics education that is "on the books" in the various provinces. It is important to note, however, that there can often be a substantial difference between what is in the curriculum, what teachers actually teach and what students actually learn. Teachers have considerable freedom to present curricular material in the way they see fit. Most high school teachers in Canada have no formal training in political science and they often rely heavily on their textbooks for material to present to students. Texts used are often not "special-purpose" books devoted to government and politics, but general-purpose social studies or history books. Lowering the voting age would provide an opportunity for schools to bring an immediacy to their political education that is now lacking. It would also offer an opportunity for boards of education to re-examine their social studies curricula as to their adequacy in the area of voting and elections. Where courses are available in high schools giving the basics of civics education with regard to elections, little impact on the curriculum would be expected from a change in the voting age. Where courses are not available, their development would be required, but given the existence of models in many other places, this should not be difficult.

Lowering the voting age would also necessitate the development of rules to regulate political campaigning in schools, should elections take place during the school term. In most (perhaps all) provinces, the relevant education act gives the power to local school boards to restrict advertising in the schools. This would presumably include political advertising. Some school authorities might be wary of partisan clubs and active campaigning in the schools. Others may have no qualms about it. "All-candidate meetings" have been held in some high schools during recent federal and provincial elections without problems; reports indicate that attendance at these debates has gone well beyond the 18-year-olds for whom they were primarily intended. Diversification of authority to regulate political activity in the schools might result in a patchwork of different regulations; if standardization is considered desirable, new legislation might be required.

CONCLUSION

We have not considered it our role in this study to act as advocates for lowering the voting age or to advise against the move. Rather, we have tried to systematize the arguments made on both sides of the issue and to assemble data that might bear on the potential consequences. Our overall conclusion is that, whereas this reform would engender considerable public debate, it would be a low-risk endeavour, in the sense that it would not produce a major impact on the political process or the high schools.

We estimate that approximately 50 to 60 percent of 16- and 17-year-olds would vote if given the opportunity. Although this age group is not currently demanding the vote en masse, there is cautious support for the change among the relevant age group and among other young people. There is no reason to believe that the voting patterns of 16- and 17-year-olds would be appreciably different from the electorate in general. We do not envisage a major impact on schools, unless the curriculum in some places contains no civics education. Some campaigning activity in schools could be expected and would need to be regulated. Increased classroom discussion of election issues could be expected.

APPENDIX
POLITICAL EDUCATION IN CANADIAN SCHOOLS

Province	Course title	Grade	Status
Alberta	Social Studies	6	Compulsory
	Social Studies	10	Compulsory
	Political Thinking	11	Optional
	Comparative Government	11	Optional
	Social Studies	12	Compulsory
	International Relations	12	Optional
British Columbia	Social Studies	6	Compulsory
	Social Studies	11	Compulsory
	Law	12	Optional
Manitoba	Social Studies	9	Compulsory
	Canadian History	11	Compulsory
	World Issues	12	Optional
New Brunswick	Social Studies	6	Compulsory
	Social Studies	7–8	Compulsory
	Maritime Studies	10	Optional
	Political Science	12	Optional
Newfoundland	Social Studies	3–7	Compulsory
	Social Studies	9	Compulsory
	Canadian Issues	10	Optional
	Democracy	11	Compulsory
Northwest Territories	Civics	6–10	Compulsory
	Northern Studies	11–12	Compulsory
	Social Studies	10–12	Compulsory
Nova Scotia	Social Studies	7	Compulsory
	Social Studies	8	Compulsory
	Social Studies	9	Compulsory
	Political Science	12	Optional
Ontario	Citizenship: Government and Law	10–12	Optional
	Politics	OAC	Optional
Prince Edward Island	Political Studies	11	Optional
	Political Studies	12	Optional
	Canadian History	12	Optional
Quebec	No courses on politics in high schools. Optional courses can be taken in Cegeps.		
Saskatchewan	Political Science	12	Optional
	Canadian Studies	12	Compulsory
Yukon	Social Studies	8–11	Compulsory

Alberta

Course listings are deceptive about the extent to which school students are exposed to the study of politics. The compulsory courses offer the most instruction to Albertan students. The grade 6 Social Studies course devotes one-third of its instruction to local government. The grade 10 Social Studies course has half of its instruction on the topics of citizenship, civil rights and government structures. According to 1988–89 figures, the optional courses are greatly underused. The Political Thinking course saw only 22 students, and Comparative Government, only 77 students. The International Relations course did somewhat better with a reported figure of 469.

British Columbia

The grade 6 Social Studies course contains a component concerning politics and government. The grade 11 Social Studies course has 25 hours of instruction about Canadian government, representation and ideologies. The grade 12 Law course contains 12 000 students.

Manitoba

The grade 9 Social Studies course has an emphasis on Canada and includes a study of Canadian government that incorporates the use of an "Elections Kit," probably containing material from Elections Canada. The Canadian History course contains a section on the history of government. The World Issues optional course is taken by approximately one-third of Manitoban grade 12 students. In this course there is coverage of different systems of government and ideology.

New Brunswick

The Social Studies courses from grades 6 to 8 cover some topics related to understanding politics. The grade 6 course covers three major topics, one of which is the study of government. Grades 7 and 8 contain a survey course on history up to the 1950s, and one component of this course is how government in Canada evolved. In the Maritime Studies course, taken by an estimated 60 percent of students at the grade 10 level, there is some discussion related to issues of political power in society. The grade 12 Political Science course is undergoing some revision by the Department of Education. Its current enrolment is low: less than 1 000 of approximately 5 000 eligible grade 12 students.

Newfoundland

The political studies content offered in Newfoundland reaches back to the very early grades under the Social Studies course umbrella. Grade 3 children are given selected community case studies, such as a look at the Council of Fogo Island. Grade 5 students study their province's history and the debates over Newfoundland's entry into Canada. Grade 6 students concentrate on Canada, and grade 7 students study the North American continent. Grade 7 also has some study of the Canadian electoral process. In the grade 9 course there is a study of Canadian Confederation and developments in Canada's political history.

The Democracy course is currently under review and may become optional. An estimated 2 500 students (mostly at the grade 11 level) now take the course, which covers the meaning of democracy, political organizations, political participation and federal-provincial relations. The Canadian Issues course (chiefly for grade 10 students) deals with various political, economic and social relations issues and includes a discussion on political participation and the lobbying process. The enrolment figures for this course are small: less than 500 of a possible estimated 3 000 students take the course. Changes in the school curriculum may increase the enrolment figures.

Northwest Territories

The Social Studies program is being revised in the Northwest Territories. Currently, there is a program entitled Civics that is taught from grade 6 to grade 11. The relevant course is usually entitled Civics, but not always. The grades 10–12 Social Studies courses are based on Alberta's social studies program. The Northern Studies course has some instruction on government processes and institutions. Also discussed are forms of Aboriginal governance.

Nova Scotia

Social Studies for the grade 7–9 levels has a component entitled Civics. For grade 7, the civics component focuses on the municipal level of politics. Grade 8 looks at the provincial level; grade 9, at Maritime and federal politics. It should be noted that Nova Scotia is the only province that offers what seems to be a coherent multiyear program for the study of politics. The grade 12 Political Science course is optional and has an estimated 1 200 students of a possible 8 000–9 000. Material for this course includes information from Elections Canada.

Ontario

The courses in political studies are offered as optional courses at the high school level. Very little is offered at the primary and junior levels (up to grade 6). At the high school level the Citizenship: Government and Law course is compulsory, the level of instruction varying from basic to advanced. The content of this course deals with federal elections, voting, and forms of political participation. It is unclear how many students are registered in the optional Politics courses, which aim to give an academic introduction to political science.

Prince Edward Island

At the junior high school level in the history program there is a 10 percent component entitled Civics. Most courses in political studies occur at the high school level and all three are listed as optional. The grade 11 Political Studies course has an estimated 10–15 percent of possible students. The grade 12 Political Studies course has an estimated 6 percent of students. The Canadian History course, also optional, has a larger enrolment, but still only 25–35 percent. One of the texts used for this course is Irwin's *How We Are Governed in the 90s.* Since the program for social studies is currently being refashioned, enrolment figures may change in the next year or two.

Quebec

According to the Information Bureau of the Quebec Ministry of Education, at the secondary level no courses are offered devoted to politics, but some coverage of politics may be given in geography and history courses. Courses in politics can be taken at the Cegep level (roughly equivalent to academically oriented grades 12 and 13 in other provinces).

Saskatchewan

The Political Studies course in Saskatchewan is an animal of many stripes. The course label varies in some schools. Its general content consists of politics, government systems, history, and organizational forms of representation and activity. Although a grade 12 course, it is sometimes offered at the grade 11 level. Not compulsory, it is offered in most schools located in urban and major centres. For this province, this means a minority of institutions offer it. Roughly 50 percent of grade 12 students have the opportunity to take this course. Canadian Studies is compulsory, as it is under the Social Studies umbrella of courses. At this time it is part of a revised structure, meaning that the year the students started school determines whether they will have to take the course.

Yukon

The Yukon curriculum is borrowed from the BC course system; however, some changes have been made to accommodate the different educational needs of Yukon students. The grade 8 Social Studies course, which focuses mainly on history, has 15–20 percent of its content devoted to current affairs. The grade 9 course has some discussion of First Nations issues and developments regarding the *Constitution Act, 1867.* It also covers issues of industrialization and its social effects. The grade 10 course looks at Confederation and developments pertaining to the West and North, and the territories and their political evolution. Lastly, in grade 11, 30 percent of the course is devoted to instruction on government and law, including a study of the Canadian political and electoral system.

NOTES

1. Material compiled by Richard S. Katz, Johns Hopkins University, for forthcoming publication.

2. *The Gallup Report*, 31 January 1970.

REFERENCES

Canada. House of Commons. 1969. *Debates*, 23 October.

————. 1970. *Debates*, 27 May–25 June.

Clarke, Harold D., Jane Jenson, Lawrence LeDuc and Jon H. Pammett. 1991. *Absent Mandate: Interpreting Change in Canadian Elections.* 2d ed. Toronto: Gage.

Conley, Marshall. 1988. "Political Education in the Schools: A View from Atlantic Canada." In *Political Education in Canada*, ed. Jon H. Pammett and Jean-Luc Pepin. Halifax: Institute for Research on Public Policy.

Garant, Patrice. 1991. "Revisiting the Voting Age Issue under the *Canadian Charter of Rights and Freedoms.*" In *Youth in Canadian Politics: Participation and Involvement*, ed. Kathy Megyery. Vol. 8 of the research studies of the Royal Commission on Electoral Reform and Party Financing. Ottawa and Toronto: RCERPF/Dundurn.

Hudon, Raymond, Bernard Fournier, Louis Métivier, with the assistance of Benoît-Paul Hébert. 1991. "To What Extent Are Today's Young People Interested in Politics? Inquiries among 16- to 24-Year-Olds." In *Youth in Canadian Politics: Participation and Involvement*, ed. Kathy Megyery. Vol. 8 of the research studies of the Royal Commission on Electoral Reform and Party Financing. Ottawa and Toronto: RCERPF/Dundurn.

Mercier, Jean. 1988. "L'apprentissage politique des jeunes Québécois dans les écoles." In *Political Education in Canada*, ed. Jon H. Pammett and Jean-Luc Pepin. Halifax: Institute for Research on Public Policy.

Milbrath, Lester. 1965. *Political Participation: How and Why Do People Get Involved in Politics?* Chicago: Rand McNally.

Mishler, William. 1979. *Political Participation in Canada*. Toronto: Gage.

Osborne, Ken. 1988. "Political Education in the Schools of Western Canada." In *Political Education in Canada*, ed. Jon H. Pammett and Jean-Luc Pepin. Halifax: Institute for Research on Public Policy.

Pammett, Jon H. 1991. "Voting Turnout in Canada." In *Voter Turnout in Canada*, ed. Herman Bakvis. Vol. 15 of the research studies of the Royal Commission on Electoral Reform and Party Financing. Ottawa and Toronto: RCERPF/Dundurn.

Ricker, John, and John Saywell. 1991. *How We Are Governed in the 90s.* Toronto: Irwin.

CONTRIBUTORS TO VOLUME 8

Bernard Fournier	Université Laval
Patrice Garant	Université Laval
Benoît-Paul Hébert	Université Laval
Raymond Hudon	Université Laval
Louis Métivier	Université Laval
John Myles	Carleton University
Jon H. Pammett	Carleton University

ACKNOWLEDGEMENTS

The Royal Commission on Electoral Reform and Party Financing and the publishers wish to acknowledge with gratitude the permission of the following to reprint and translate material:

Association canadienne-française pour l'avancement des sciences.

Care has been taken to trace the ownership of copyright material used in the text, including the tables and figures. The authors and publishers welcome any information enabling them to rectify any reference or credit in subsequent editions.

~

Consistent with the Commission's objective of promoting full participation in the electoral system by all segments of Canadian society, gender neutrality has been used wherever possible in the editing of the research studies.

THE COLLECTED RESEARCH STUDIES*

_____

* The titles of studies may not be final in all cases.

VOLUME 9

Aboriginal Peoples and Electoral Reform in Canada
Robert A. Milen, Editor

ROBERT A. MILEN — Aboriginal Constitutional and Electoral Reform

AUGIE FLERAS — Aboriginal Electoral Districts for Canada: Lessons from New Zealand

VALERIE ALIA — Aboriginal Peoples and Campaign Coverage in the North

ROGER GIBBINS — Electoral Reform and Canada's Aboriginal Population: An Assessment of Aboriginal Electoral Districts

VOLUME 10

Democratic Rights and Electoral Reform in Canada
Michael Cassidy, Editor

JENNIFER SMITH — The Franchise and Theories of Representative Government

PIERRE LANDREVILLE AND LUCIE LEMONDE — Voting Rights for Inmates

YVES DENONCOURT — Reflections concerning Criteria for the Vote for Persons with Mental Disorders

PATRICE GARANT — Political Rights of Public Servants in the Political Process

KENNETH KERNAGHAN — The Political Rights of Canada's Federal Public Servants

PETER MCCORMICK — Provision for the Recall of Elected Officials: Parameters and Prospects

DAVID MAC DONALD — Referendums and Federal General Elections

JOHN C. COURTNEY AND DAVID E. SMITH — Registering Voters: Canada in a Comparative Context

CÉCILE BOUCHER — Administration and Enforcement of the Elections Act in Canada

VOLUME 11

Drawing the Map: Equality and Efficacy of the Vote in Canadian Electoral Boundary Reform
David Small, Editor

VOLUME 12

Political Ethics: A Canadian Perspective
Janet Hiebert, Editor

VOLUME 19
Media, Elections and Democracy
  Frederick J. Fletcher, Editor

JACQUES GERSTLÉ	Election Communication in France
HOLLI A. SEMETKO	Broadcasting and Election Communication in Britain
KLAUS SCHOENBACH	Mass Media and Election Campaigns in Germany
KAREN SIUNE	Campaign Communication in Scandinavia
JOHN WARHURST	Campaign Communication in Australian Elections
DORIS A. GRABER	The Mass Media and Election Campaigns in the United States of America
FREDERICK J. FLETCHER AND ROBERT EVERETT	Mass Media and Elections in Canada

VOLUME 20
Reaching the Voter: Constituency Campaigning in Canada
  David V. J. Bell and Frederick J. Fletcher, Editors

DAVID V.J. BELL AND FREDERICK J. FLETCHER	Electoral Communication at the Constituency Level: A Framework for Analysis
ANTHONY M. SAYERS	Local Issue Space at National Elections: Kootenay West–Revelstoke and Vancouver Centre
ANDREW BEH AND ROGER GIBBINS	The Campaign–Media Interface in Local Constituencies: Two Alberta Case Studies from the 1988 Federal Election Campaign
DAVID V.J. BELL AND CATHERINE M. BOLAN	The Mass Media and Federal Election Campaigning at the Local Level: A Case Study of Two Ontario Constituencies
LUC BERNIER	Local Campaigns and the Media: The 1988 Election in Outremont and Frontenac
LEONARD PREYRA	Riding the Waves: Parties, the Media and the 1988 Federal Election in Nova Scotia

VOLUME 23
Canadian Political Parties in the Constituencies:
A Local Perspective

R. KENNETH CARTY · Canadian Political Parties in the
Constituencies: A Local Perspective

COMMISSION ORGANIZATION

CHAIRMAN
Pierre Lortie

COMMISSIONERS
Pierre Fortier
Robert Gabor
William Knight
Lucie Pépin

SENIOR OFFICERS

Executive Director
Guy Goulard

Director of Research
Peter Aucoin

Special Adviser to the Chairman
Jean-Marc Hamel

Research
F. Leslie Seidle,
  Senior Research Coordinator

Coordinators
Herman Bakvis
Michael Cassidy
Frederick J. Fletcher
Janet Hiebert
Kathy Megyery
Robert A. Milen
David Small

Assistant Coordinators
David Mac Donald
Cheryl D. Mitchell

Legislation
Jules Brière, Senior Adviser
Gérard Bertrand
Patrick Orr

Communications and Publishing
Richard Rochefort, Director
Hélène Papineau, Assistant
  Director
Paul Morisset, Editor
Kathryn Randle, Editor

Finance and Administration
Maurice R. Lacasse, Director

Contracts and Personnel
Thérèse Lacasse, Chief

Editorial, Design and Production Services

Royal Commission on Electoral Reform and Party Financing

Editors   Denis Bastien, Susan Becker Davidson, Ginette Bertrand, Louis Bilodeau, Claude Brabant, Louis Chabot, Danielle Chaput, Norman Dahl, Carlos del Burgo, Julie Desgagners, Chantal Granger, Volker Junginger, Denis Landry, André LaRose, Paul Morisset, Christine O'Meara, Mario Pelletier, Marie-Noël Pichelin, Kathryn Randle, Georges Royer, Eve Valiquette, Dominique Vincent.

Le Centre de Documentation Juridique du Québec Inc.

Hubert Reid, *President*

Claire Grégoire, *Comptroller*

Lucie Poirier, *Production Manager*
Gisèle Gingras, *Special Project Assistant*

Translators   Pierre-Yves de la Garde, Richard Lapointe, Marie-Josée Turcotte.

Technical Editors   Stéphane Côté Coulombe, *Coordinator*;
Josée Chabot, Danielle Morin.

Copy Editors   Martine Germain, Lise Larochelle, Elisabeth Reid, Carole St-Louis, Isabelle Tousignant, Charles Tremblay, Sébastien Viau.

Word Processing   André Vallée.

Formatting   Typoform, Claude Audet; Linda Goudreau, *Formatting Coordinator.*

Wilson & Lafleur Ltée

Claude Wilson, *President*